A CENTURY FOR
THE CENTURY

HUTNER · KELLY

A CENTURY

FINE PRINTED BOOKS

FOR THE

FROM 1900 TO 1999

CENTURY

THE GROLIER CLUB &

DAVID R. GODINE 2004

This revised and enlarged edition published in 2004 by

DAVID R. GODINE, *Publisher*

Post Office Box 450

Jaffrey, New Hampshire 03452

www.godine.com

LIBRARY OF CONGRESS CATALOGING-IN-PUBLICATION DATA

Hutner, Martin.

A century for the century : fine printed books from 1900 to 1999 /
by Martin Hutner & Jerry Kelly.—Rev. and enl. ed.

p.   cm.

Includes bibliographical references and index.

ISBN 1-56792-220-1 (hardcover : alk. paper)

1. Fine books—Europe—Bibliography—Exhibitions.

2. Fine books—United States—Bibliography—Exhibitions.

3. Private press books—Europe—Bibliography—Exhibitions.

4. Private press books—United States—Bibliography—Exhibitions.

1. Kelly, Jerry, 1955– 11. Title.

Z1033.F5H87 2004

015.4—dc22

2004019023

Revised Edition 2004
Printed in China by C & C Offset

CONTENTS

FOREWORD

SIGNIFICANT ANNIVERSARY YEARS evoke an almost instinctive desire for summation and evaluation. The end of a century brings such considerations to an almost fever pitch. Lists of twentieth-century achievements appeared with regularity in the late 1990s. What could be more appropriate for the Grolier Club than a century of books for a century of years? Yet the idea of choosing one hundred books from all the superlative books of the twentieth century is daunting. Can one choose only one hundred books for their beauty from so many thousands? Consider that the American Institute of Graphic Arts celebrates fifty superb books each year. Since 1928, when the AIGA book show started, there has been a cumulative total of 3,600 selections. The idea of one book a year, on average, seems almost presumptuous. Yet one must begin somewhere and celebrate the chosen, rather than lament the many left unsung.

This survey includes only books printed from the greco-roman alphabets in Europe and America. We have also limited ourselves to the book in the traditional sense, leaving aside "book objects" and other more sculptural works where the traditional function of the book has been relegated to a secondary role. We have, however, considered the book as a whole – with all the elements – from typography and paper through presswork and binding – taken into account.

From the outset, the process of selection went well for us, the curators, as our first lists for each other's perusal showed that we had chosen the same seventy-one books out of one hundred. This early consensus gave us the confidence to discuss, evaluate, and choose the rest. After many more or less obvious choices, the remaining selections proved difficult. Several fine volumes remained under consideration up to the last minute. We sought the counsel of interested friends (thanked below) who made suggestions – some of which were acted upon, some not – with the final decisions being ours.

We have divided the century between us, so that the introduction is comprised of two essays. The first half covers the years through World War II, and the second brings us to the present. On the following pages are some of the most beautiful, finely printed books produced during the twentieth century arranged in chronological order. We hope that the viewer – and reader – will find old favorites and come to appreciate new ones.

MH & JK

ACKNOWLEDGMENTS

A BOOK such as this will always rely on the efforts of many people aside from the authors. Space will not permit us to thank here all who have helped, but we will take this opportunity to acknowledge several people whose assistance is greatly appreciated. Greer Allen, Kenneth A. Auchincloss, Paul Barnes, Francis O. Mattson, and David Pankow helped early on in the selection process. Assistance with loans for the exhibition and photographs for reproduction was generously given by Virginia Bartow, Jennifer Lee, Robert Rainwater, and Margaret Glover at the New York Public Library and Andrew Robison at the National Gallery.

The efforts of our colleagues at the Grolier Club – Carol Rothkopf, Eric Holzenberg, and Michael North – were invaluable in the preparation of the catalogue. All photographs are by Robert Lorenzson except nos. 1, 29, 43, 45, 49, 55, 79, 86, and 92,, which are courtesy of the New York Public Library; no. 96 courtesy of the Gehenna Press; no. 94 courtesy of the Gilman Paper Company; no. 44 courtesy of the National Gallery of Art; no. 76 courtesy of the Melbert B. Cary, Jr. Graphic Arts Collection; and no. 100, photograph by D. James Dee, courtesy of Vincent FitzGerald & Co.

Special thanks to our friend David R. Godine for publishing the trade edition of this book, which we trust will expose a wider audience to the range and accomplishments of book typography in the twentieth century.

THE RESURGENCE OF FINE PRINTING:
TRADITION AND CHANGE, 1900–1949

AS THE NINETEENTH CENTURY moved to its close, a reevaluation of printing was underway that was to have a profound effect upon printing in the next century. I refer, of course, to the work of William Morris (1834–1896) in England, whose career in the decorative arts was capped by the extraordinary influence of his Kelmscott Press. Yet it is ironic that the far-reaching influence of Morris's work harked back, in style, to the Middle Ages. How can a seemingly outdated style be considered revolutionary or modern? In Morris's case, *style* must be separated from *method*. Morris's concern with the debased Victorianized style into which printing had increasingly sunk by the late 1880s caused him to look to the past for ideas that were to become an impetus for the future, in much the same way as his artist colleagues were doing in the Pre-Raphaelite Movement. Morris was already involved – and was in many ways the seminal force – in the corresponding Arts and Crafts Movement that grew out of a distaste for machine-made objects. During the Victorian period, industrialized manufacturing processes naturally affected the decorative arts. In addition, a paucity of artistic invention – with the exception of a few figures of genius and taste such as Augustus Welby Pugin – ushered in a period of shoddily made, poorly designed work. Long before Morris founded his Kelmscott Press in 1891, he was designing furniture, wallpaper, and fabrics, to be produced by his own company, utilizing hand techniques or manufactured under his supervision.

In 1888, a friend of Morris's, Emery Walker (1851–1933), a technician and printer, gave a lecture at an Arts and Crafts exhibition in London of photographic enlargements of typefaces from the early days of printing (the fifteenth and sixteenth centuries). Morris attended this lecture and resolved to embark on yet another enterprise – fine printing. Together, Morris and Walker initiated the creation of new types – antiquarian in inspiration – determined to raise standards of printing as high as possible. Repeatedly throughout the 1890s, and well into the twentieth century, the passion for type based upon the earlier great types was to go hand-in-hand with the formation of new presses and new ideas of printing. Morris could not entirely escape the heavily patterned, complicated, often excessively elaborate style so beloved by his fellow Victorians, who often took their inspiration from the Gothic and Renaissance eras. With Morris, however, an insistence on quality, the devotion to excellence in every component of printing – typography, paper, ink, presswork – provided the elements of revolution. In less than a decade, Morris's example had turned printing on its head, and avid disciples were turning out work that ultimately emerged from its medievalized chrysalis into something quite modern. After Morris's death in 1896 (the year of the publication of his masterpiece, *The Works of Geoffrey Chaucer*), the wave of interest in fine printing continued unabated. Emery Walker remained a seminal figure whose interest and involvement in other presses proved a great factor in their successes. It was

Walker's collaboration with T. J. Cobden-Sanderson and the formation of the Doves Press in 1900, that at its very outset quietly set the tone for the twentieth century.

This essay is meant to act as an introduction to the books that comprised our exhibition, and while the exhibits are presented chronologically, some of the presses, designers, or printers may have begun their work earlier than those cited. Given the limitations of space our essays cannot be a full history of modern printed books in the western world, but rather a personal overview of what we feel was some of the best work produced in each of the two halves of the century.

1   In some ways *Parallèlement*, printed in France, of 1900 (no. 1) is the perfect book with which to start our analysis of printing in the twentieth century, for even today it seems very "modern" with its bold, elegant, innovative design of text printed over illustration. It seems light years distant from the medievalized designs of the Kelmscott Press and its imitators. At the time of its design and publication, Pierre Bonnard (1867–1947) was still a young artist, emerging from the influence of Post-Impressionism in France. In this book he combined illustrations and text in a wholly new way, with the letterforms and rose-colored lithographs having an equal and complementary duality.

In England, the Ashendene Press (founded 1894) and Doves Press (established 1900) had been created as the result of the widespread influence of the Kelmscott Press. T. J. Cobden-Sanderson (1840–1922), of the Doves Press and the Doves Bindery, started life as a barrister and had been a friend of William Morris. After giving up the law, he took up bookbinding, in which he excelled, and ultimately formed a printing partnership with Emery Walker. Like Morris, he developed his own proprietary types with Walker. Unlike those of Morris and the Kelmscott Press, his books were unillustrated, spare, and only rarely adorned with calligraphic flourishes. Edward

6   Johnston's flourishes in *Men and Women* (1908, no. 6), or the occasional capital letter such as the

4   magisterial "I" (also by Johnston) which begins *The English Bible* (1903–1905, no. 4), are perfect examples. All of the Doves Press work is notable for the clarity, simplicity, even purity, of its printing. And while the types hark back to Nicolas Jenson, the books look modern. The work of the Ashendene Press, on the other hand, with its own proprietary type, was frequently illus-

3   trated, often superbly, as shown in the Dante (1902, no. 3). The books, sometimes large productions, are more Renaissance in feeling than modern. Handsomely printed, often on vellum as well as on paper, these books form a sizable and elegant body of work that continued under C. H. St. John Hornby (1867–1946), the press's proprietor, until its close in 1935. The Ashendene

35   Press's *Bibliography* (1935, no. 35) exhibits all the strengths of the press, even as it enumerated all their work printed to date.

At the same time in Britain, Lucien Pissarro (1863–1944), the son of the great French painter, Camille Pissarro, and Lucien's wife, Esther, established their Eragny Press. Pissarro had purchased a handpress in 1894 and began printing books using Charles Ricketts's Vale Press type. The Vale Press was active in England at the end of the century. Unlike Morris and Ricketts, who never actually printed at their presses, the Pissarros jointly designed their books and illustrations, engraved woodblocks, set the type, and personally printed them. By 1903, when Camille

Pissarro died, Lucien had finished the design for his own typeface, Brook, which his father had subsidized. The last sixteen books of the Eragny Press, including the beautiful *Songs by Ben Jonson* (1906, no. 5), are set in Brook and contain woodcuts printed in multiple colors. 5

The next generation of printers and designers, all of whom were also born in the late nineteenth century, are represented in the exhibition. Many of these practitioners were drawn to subjects in printing history, as a number of the following books indicate. Stanley Morison (1889–1967) was to become one of the great lights of British printing as a designer, typographer, and historian. One of Morison's lasting accomplishments was his design of the Times New Roman type, which revolutionized the look of the London *Times*, and is still in general use. In 1930 Morison wrote and designed the elegant *John Bell* (no. 24), on the eighteenth-century 24 printer, for the Cambridge University Press. As a result of Morris's and Walker's investigations, printing scholarship had become the subject of much printing production. Besides Morison's work on Bell, there were a number of other noteworthy books, such as George W. Jones's (1860–1942) handsomely produced volumes on printing history – one of the finest being *Henri & Robert Estienne* (1929, no. 17), printed at "The Sign of the Dolphin" in London. 17

For 1931, we chose two books by the multitalented Eric Gill (1882–1940), an artist equally proficient as sculptor, stonecutter, wood-engraver, book and type designer. *The Four Gospels* (1931, no. 26) from the Golden Cockerel Press – a press that was to have a notable printing his- 26 tory – is certainly among the more beautiful books produced in England, printed with Gill's own type and illustrations. It is shown alongside *An Essay on Typography* (1931, no. 28), produced 28 in collaboration with his son-in-law, René Hague.

Another of Britain's important printing enterprises, the Curwen Press, enjoyed one of the country's longest and most distinguished histories. In the 1920s, Oliver Simon (1895–1956) joined the press, and under his direction it developed into one of Britain's finest, most diversified presses. Simon was a founder of the great typographic journal, *The Fleuron*. In 1932, the press produced one of its masterpieces, the *Urne Buriall* (no. 30), with illustrations by Paul Nash. 30

Despite the effects of the depression and the approach of war, two presses, one in London and the other in Wales, were able to produce three great books. In 1933, the Nonesuch Press, established in London in 1923 under the directorship of Francis Meynell (1891–1975), produced its great seven-volume *Works of Shakespeare* (no. 33), and *The Nonesuch Century* (no. 38), an ap- 33, 38 praisal and bibliography of the press, was printed in 1936. The private Gregynog Press in rural Wales produced its magnificent *The History of St. Louis* in 1937 (no. 40). The press's first phase 40 ended in 1940 while the country was at war.

In the United States, printing in the last quarter of the nineteenth century was dominated by the work of Theodore Low De Vinne (1828–1914), a founder and early president of the Grolier Club, who strove diligently to improve the quality of American printing. A scholar-printer in the old Renaissance tradition, De Vinne wrote works on printing history as well as producing fine and job printing. Born in 1828, he died in 1914 after a long and successful career. His work was always meticulously printed, if not always highly imaginative, but his *Title-Pages as Seen by*

2 *a Printer* of 1901 (no. 2), produced for the Grolier Club, marries the best of his scholarship and skill, and shows the work of his press at its acme.

Thomas Bird Mosher (1852–1923) began his career as publisher and printer in Portland, Maine, in 1891, the same year as the founding of the Kelmscott Press. Mosher had had several careers before settling down to publishing at the age of thirty-nine. Unlike the works of the Kelmscott Press, Mosher's books were mostly executed in small formats, well designed and well printed, and priced to be attractive to a larger public. Occasionally, he would produce 8 deluxe volumes in limited editions such as the Calvert in 1913 (no. 8). In a career that lasted until 1923, Mosher produced more than four hundred books of consistent quality.

By now, American presses were producing work equal to that being done in Europe. Much fine work emanated from Daniel Berkeley Updike's Merrymount Press. Having modestly begun a career as an office boy at Houghton Mifflin in Boston, and later at the Riverside Press in Cambridge, Updike (1860–1941) went on to found his press in Boston in 1893. At first heavily influenced by Morris and the Kelmscott Press, the Merrymount Press was to become one of the longest-lived (fifty-six years) and most distinguished presses in America in the first half of the 9 twentieth century. *Newark* (1917, no. 9), Washington Irving's *Notes and Journal of Travel in Europe* 10, 25 (1921, no. 10) and the press's masterpiece, *The Book of Common Prayer* (no. 25), exhibit the elegance, superb design, scholarship, and printing that embody the best of American work.

Ten years younger than Updike, Bruce Rogers (1870–1957), a young artist from Indiana, began his career in the last decade of the nineteenth century and followed on Updike's heels to join the Riverside Press in 1896. Rogers went from strength to strength (as he was to go from press to press) designing one great book after another, variously in America and England, where 7 his work was also admired. Rogers's *Geofroy Tory* (1909, no. 7), printed at the Riverside Press, his 32, 34 *Odyssey* (1932, no. 32), the *Fra Luca de Pacioli* (1933, no. 34) for the Grolier Club, and the majestic 37 lectern *Holy Bible* of 1935 (no. 37), show him at his peak as artist, typographer, and designer. In many ways, Updike and Rogers were the two great pillars of American printing of the first half of the twentieth century. As different as they could possibly be in temperament and personality – Rogers, the independent, peripatetic, elegant artist-designer, and Updike, the steadfast, conservative, devout scholar-printer – they both helped to raise the craft of printing in America to an art form.

From the end of the nineteenth century onward, fine printing was produced all over the country. New England, New York, Chicago, and San Francisco played host to emerging and energetic small printing enterprises, all striving to produce beautiful works for an eager public. John Henry Nash (1871–1947) arrived in San Francisco in 1895 and started to work as a compositor, employed by some of the city's best printing houses before forming a relationship with the 41 established firm of Taylor & Taylor whose excellent *Types Borders and Miscellany* (1939, no. 41) is shown here. In 1911, at the age of forty, Nash set up his own printing business. Although his productions were always beautifully printed, his style was frequently as blustery and florid as his personality. But Nash was capable of elegance and restraint, as displayed in his four-volume 18 *The Divine Comedy* of Dante printed in 1929 (no. 18).

The next generation of San Francisco printers is represented by the Grabhorn brothers and their press. Edwin (1890–1968) and his brother Robert (1900–1973) began their press in 1920. Drawn from their native Indianapolis by San Francisco's burgeoning printing industry, they ultimately settled there, and over their long careers produced some of the finest printing to come from the West Coast. In 1930, they printed Whitman's *Leaves of Grass* (no. 23), in an edition that has achieved lasting fame. The press continued until 1965, having had a distinguished life of forty-five years, during which they produced their first great Grabhorn *Bibliography* (1940, no. 42), followed by subsequent bibliographies in 1957 and 1977.

23

42

In Chicago, the hub of fine printing in the Midwest, such small publishers as Stone and Kimball and Way and Williams, flourished at the turn of the century. R. R. Donnelley's Lakeside Press printed for many of these smaller enterprises, and produced their own noteworthy series of American Classics, including *Moby-Dick* in 1930 (no. 22) illustrated by Rockwell Kent. In one way or another, Donnelly dominated the Chicago printing scene for the entire century.

22

On the East Coast, Elmer Adler (1884–1961), a talented printer, designer, editor, publisher, and collector born in Rochester, New York, in 1884, left the family clothing business to set up a print shop in 1922 in New York City. He named it the Pynson Printers in honor of the early Anglo-Norman printer, Richard Pynson (d. 1530). In its eighteen years the press printed many superb books, often in conjunction with Random House. In 1929, under his own imprint, Adler produced the splendid volume, *The Decorative Work of T. M. Cleland* (no. 19). Cleland was a book designer and artist who had his own turn-of-the-century press, later doing commissioned work, notably for the Merrymount Press. From the many fine publications published by the Typophiles we chose a charming and beautifully printed small-scale conceit, *Diggings from many ampersand-hogs*. It combines the typographical work of a large number of American printers and designers, all of whom contributed whimsical compositions based on the ampersand (1936, no. 39).

19

39

As the advent of printing had taken place in Germany in the mid-fifteenth century – together with an equally long and distinguished tradition of woodcut illustration – it is not surprising to find the revival of the book arts as rich there as in the rest of Europe and America. Germany, to a greater extent than other countries, profited from state-supported arts and crafts schools in most of its major cities. All the book arts were taught in these schools, providing a host of young artisans for the emerging commercial and private presses. Foremost among these figures was Rudolf Koch (1876–1934), who was involved with the arts and crafts school in Offenbach. There he attracted talented disciples who went on to become major figures in their own right. Koch, like Morris, was a man of many talents – artist, designer, typographer. His striking *Die Vier Evangelien* (1926, no. 16) and elegant *Das Blumenbuch* (1929–1930, no. 20) are among the glories of German fine printing.

16, 20

One of the greatest of the German private presses was the Bremer Presse established in 1911 by Willy Wiegand (1884–1961), the son of an industrialist, whose press continued printing up to the beginning of the World War II. All of the Bremer Presse's works were marked by superb craftsmanship, scholarship, and artistry. The Dante (1921, no. 11), the two-volume Homer (1923–1924, no. 12), and St. Augustine's *De Civitate Dei* (1925, no. 14) are among the most beauti-

11

12, 14

ful. These books are magnificently printed in Bremer Presse proprietary types and unadorned save for initial letters created by Anna Simons – a pupil and disciple of Edward Johnston.

The second of the great German private presses was the Cranach Presse, begun by Count Harry Kessler (1868–1937) in Weimar in 1913. During World War I the press was directed by the Belgian designer, Henry van de Velde. After the war, Kessler cast his net to other countries, 15 commissioning major artists to illustrate his books. Virgil's *Eclogues* (1926, no. 15) boasted superb woodcuts by Aristide Maillol, with a title page and initial letters by Eric Gill, a roman type 21 produced by Emery Walker, and an italic by Edward Johnston. *The Tragedie of Hamlet* (1929–1930, no. 21) (which was preceded by a German edition in the same format) had woodcuts by 29 Edward Gordon Craig, and the *Canticum Canticorum* of 1931 (no. 29), wood-engraved illustrations and initial letters by Eric Gill. The press ceased operations the next year when Count Kessler was forced to flee the Nazis.

At the age of twenty-four, Hans (later Giovanni) Mardersteig (1892–1977) left his native Germany for Switzerland in 1916 for reasons of health. During the World War I he worked as an editor, and then in book production for the Munich publisher Kurt Wolff. In 1922, he set up a hand press in Montagnola, Switzerland; and in 1927, he moved to Verona, having received the commission to design the forty-eight-volume edition of the works of Gabriele d'Annunzio. *Das* 13 *Roemische Carneval* of Goethe (1924, no. 13) produced during his Swiss phase, and Ovid's *Amores* 31 of 1932 (no. 31) produced in Verona at his handpress the Officina Bodoni, are two examples of the best printing by this great designer.

Another German-born designer, Jan Tschichold (1902–1974), worked in Switzerland and 36 later in England. His *Typographische Gestaltung* (1935, no. 36), with its mixture of types and its asymmetrical composition, clearly exhibits a modernist sensibility, which was shown early in Bauhaus posters and book printing. Fundamentally revolutionary in its design, such work was to push printing in a new direction, and Tschichold was one of the first and best practitioners of modernist style.

Holland is another country with a rich typographical tradition, and one where the Arts and Crafts Movement was enthusiastically embraced by many Dutch artists and artisans. Perhaps the most outstanding Dutch designer was Jan van Krimpen (1892–1958), whose type designs for the great Enschedé Foundry in Haarlem were among the most influential of the century. 27 Van Krimpen's two-volume Homer of 1931 (no. 27), printed in his handsome Romanée type, is 47 among the more beautiful books of the fertile thirties. His Psalter of 1947 (no. 47) was one of the first distinguished books to emerge after the end of World War II.

We began this survey with Verlaine's *Parallèlement,* issued in 1900, and leapfrogging four decades our survey returns to France and French printing. The French made extraordinary contributions to the arts in the first half of the twentieth century. In painting and the decorative arts they were virtually unrivaled in their industry and invention. In the book arts, it was primarily in the fields of bookbinding and in the production of *livres d'artiste* that they made their great- 43 est contribution. To demonstrate we chose Picasso's *Buffon* (1942, no. 43), Derain's *Pantagruel*

(1943, no. 45), and Matisse's *Jazz* (1947, no. 48). These are books that superlatively meld art- 45, 48
illustration, text, and printmaking. Rounding out this sampling of *livres d'artiste* is a German
publication, the rare and powerful *Apokalypse* of 1943 (no. 44) with illustration by Max Beck- 44
mann, issued by the Bauersche Giesserei in Germany.

The last book in this section of our survey is the *Esthétique du Mal* by Wallace Stevens, produced
by the Cummington Press in 1945 (no. 46). Although the press had been founded earlier at the 46
Cummington School of Art in Massachusetts, it was in 1941, as the United States entered World
War II, that Harry Duncan (1916–1997), a former English instructor and poet, joined with several leading writers, to produce the first book bearing the Cummington imprint. During the war
years, Duncan became increasingly immersed in fine printing, learning in part from the advice
and instruction of Victor Hammer (1882–1967), a book artist who had emigrated from Germany to this country. Although Duncan later moved on to Iowa and the University of Nebraska, the early books produced at Cummington were simple, dramatic, inventive, and elegant.
They helped to set the standard for the printers of the second half of the twentieth century.

Martin Hutner

THE ADVANCE OF TECHNOLOGY AND THE CONTINUITY OF TRADITION: FINE PRINTING 1949–1999

THE PRIVATE PRESS MOVEMENT, so magnificently initiated by William Morris at his Kelmscott Press (whose last book was published in 1898, therefore eliminating it from inclusion in this survey by a mere two years), was the main inspiration for many of the forty-eight selections in this book printed before 1949. Twenty-seven of those are products of a private press (meaning here that the book was printed and published by a fine press on its own account, not as a commission from a customer). One would think that the more commercial conditions of the postwar world would lead to a far greater proportion of commercial work in the fine printing arena, but surprisingly thirty-six of the selections included here from after 1949 were printed and published by fine printing establishments on their own behalf and at their own expense, not commissioned from other sources. Perhaps the growth of the publishing industry – like almost every other business – over the last fifty years has meant that only small, editorially (if not financially) independent enterprises such as the Gehenna Press in the United States or the Rampant Lions Press in England would continue to be willing to produce books that were so labor intensive and demanding, with so little potential for profit at the other end.

While Morris had initiated a revival in the art of printing that heavily influenced his immediate followers, his direct influence would dissipate and new trends in fine book design evolve after the war. Morris's overriding concern for quality materials in paper, binding, and ink, and for high levels of craftsmanship in composition and presswork has had a lasting and positive effect on the book arts, but Morris was admittedly a medievalist: he wanted his books to attain the beauty of medieval manuscripts and early printing. It should be noted, however, that he never directly copied earlier ornamentation, layout, and illustration, as many of his followers did through photoengravings and other reproductive methods. Morris's illustrations and decorations were always original, created specifically for his books. The early work of Updike and Rogers imitated Morris, but they went on to pursue different styles, still very much based on earlier periods of printing (referred to as "allusive" typography).

After 1949 there was a drive to develop a contemporary aesthetic in the book arts, using contemporary types (not merely good copies of old typefaces) in novel ways to create books that were modern and of their time while still being legible and well made. This should not be confused with the radical movements that wanted to throw away all the ideals of the past while creating a totally new look (something we are seeing again at the end of the century) – a look that appears dated today. Instead, practitioners such as Gotthard de Beauclair, Will and Sebastian Carter, Kim Merker, Hermann Zapf, and others thoroughly grounded in the classical traditions of typography created books that were beautiful and legible, yet of their time – not adaptations of early styles to modern equipment in their production techniques.

One of the overwhelming factors in printing throughout this volatile century was the march of technology. Yet only one book in this exhibition – the *Divan-E-Shams* published by Vincent FitzGerald & Company in 1996 (no. 100) – has type composed by computer-aided digital composition, and even in this instance the type was printed by letterpress from a relief surface (in this case photo-polymer plates). All other type for books included here has been cast in metal from matrices for relief letterpress printing, in much the same way as it has been done since the mid-fifteenth century. Only two or three of the pre-1949 volumes were set on a line-casting (Linotype) system and only six on the Monotype machine. Conversely, more than twenty of the postwar productions are machine set, including four set on the Linotype machine and one (mentioned above) set digitally. Perhaps the beginning of a sea change is just starting to show here, and an exhibition of finely printed books from 2000 through 2099 may include a much higher percentage of digital composition and offset lithography.

In the selection of books for this exhibition I was surprised by the consistency of production methods used in fine editions both before and after the war. Martin Hutner and I decided to divide the introductory text between us into pre-1949 books (forty-eight titles, including many in Hutner's main area of interest) and post-1949 (fifty-two titles, including many designed by typographers whose work I have studied in depth). In looking for general trends I would have expected technology to have had an increasing impact on fine bookmaking as the century progressed. Among the trends I would have anticipated were:

    1. More fine editions printed by hand before 1949

    2. More great books set by hand before 1949

    3. Fewer private press editions after 1949

    4. A significant number of books printed by offset lithography or other technologies after 1949

In fact, none of these assumptions proved true, and a remarkable consistency revealed itself in pre- and post-1949 fine book printing. Thirty-three of the pre-1949 selections were set entirely by hand, while thirty-one of the post-1949 books were hand set. Twenty-four of the books in this show printed before 1949 were printed by hand (on a hand press, or hand-fed cylinder or platen press), and virtually none involved offset lithography or other alternative methods of printing (except for artists' prints such as the lithographs in Bonnard's *Parallèlement* and Beckmann's *Apokalypse*, the pochoirs in Matisse's *Jazz*, and etchings in Picasso's *Buffon*). Again it is surprising that even more (thirty) of the post-1949 books are printed by hand. However, a dozen of the post-1949 volumes employ some amount of offset lithography, gravure, or collotype presswork. The *Amphiareo* edition (no. 81) designed by Jan Tschichold (1902–1974) and *Max Caflisch: Typographia Practica* (no. 95) printed at the Technische Hochschule Darmstadt, Germany, are the only selections printed entirely by offset lithography, and two other books are included mainly for the quality of their offset printed reproduction of photographic prints.

The survey of Caflisch's (b. 1916) work is a colorful volume utilizing the reproduction qualities of offset lithography to reproduce authentically a wide range of the work of this important typographer who did so much to raise the standards of Swiss book production.

Some books in this survey, such as the Spiral Press edition of *Chinese Calligraphy and Painting in the Collection of John M. Crawford* (1962, no. 65) and the Stamperia Valdonega's *Lo Splendore*   65
della Verona affrescata (1983, no. 91) rely to a large degree on non-letterpress printing of repro-   91
ductions for the overall beauty of the volume, while others such as the Plantin Press's *Presses of the Pacific Islands* (1967, no. 72) and the Whittington Press *Bibliography* (1982, no. 88) have only   72, 88
a few supplemental illustrations printed by offset lithography. Still, the text in all these volumes is printed by letterpress from metal type.

In this selection of exhibits no attempt was made to display technological development through the century or other changes in book production from 1900 to 1999. We found that the older technologies of handpress printing and hand-set type were employed often and effectively, even into the last decades of the century. Still, three exceptions are worth comment:

Alfred Stieglitz (1983, no. 90) published by Callaway Editions and the National Gallery of Art   90
contains seventy-three tritone reproductions of black and white photographs; one of the first instances in which images were reproduced in black and two other color inks. The third color changes through the book from a warm sepia tone to a neutral or cool black to give some sense of the variety of tone in the original prints. The 300-line screen reproductions on a textured, uncoated stock are superlatively displayed to best advantage in Eleanor Caponigro's elegant layout.

Exceptional fidelity in the printing of photographic reproductions is the *raison d'être* for another offset lithography *tour de force* in this exhibition: *Photographs from the Collection of the Gilman Paper Company* (1985, no. 94). In this instance Richard Benson painstakingly produced   94
fine line-screen negatives for each black and white image in four to six colors. The Gilman Paper Company bought and installed an offset printing press in Benson's home specifically for this project. Benson has written: "This book has always been intended to be as excellent and accurate to the originals as possible. Others have expressed this high ideal, but seldom has the attempt to achieve it been carried out on a scale such as this." The 199 plates of this impressive photo offset book bear eloquent witness to the fulfillment of this lofty goal.

It is interesting to note that while the illustrations were printed by offset lithography, the texts of both the Stieglitz and Gilman Paper Company volumes were printed by letterpress from metal type: in the case of the Stieglitz book by the Meriden-Stinehour Press in Vermont, and the Gilman by the Stamperia Valdonega in Verona, Italy.

Perhaps comparable in fidelity of reproduction, but totally different in subject and technique, is the Trianon Press facsimile of *William Blake's Water-Colour Designs for the Poems of Thomas Gray* (1972, no. 77). In three folio volumes produced over four years, the 116 pages of Blake's original   77
have been reproduced by collotype and hand coloring by means of stencils, with the text pages reproduced by letterpress from photo-engraved plates and mounted on each page by hand. Arnold Fawcus's stated goal as publisher of this book sounds strikingly similar to Benson's:

"We set ourselves the goal of absolute accuracy." Again, the printed book attests to his success.

The first books in the post-1949 part of this exhibition are the edition of Hölderlin's poems printed by Victor Hammer (1882–1967) and *Feder und Stichel* by Hermann Zapf (b. 1918), both published in 1949. *Feder und Stichel* (no. 50) was typeset in the then new Palatino font (designed by Zapf), a distinctly modern type, and arranged in a clear, open, heavily leaded style, with no ornamentation: a "modern" book. Editions were printed on elegant Japanese and Fabriano papers and hand bound using vellum or leather for the spine and handmade paper sides, or full leather for the eighty copies printed on Japanese paper. The book contains twenty-five plates of Zapf's calligraphy hand engraved in lead by August Rosenberger, meticulously printed by letterpress. A Morrisian respect for materials and craftsmanship shines through in this book, with none of the backward-looking rehashing of the private press movement.

Victor Hammer's monumental edition of Hölderlin's poems (no. 49) was set in his own distinctive uncial type, beautifully printed by hand on a sumptuous paper made to Hammer's specifications at the Magnani mill in Italy. Hammer avoided ornamentation, relying on the beauty of the letterforms elegantly presented, as is also the case with Zapf's *Feder und Stichel*. The other book in this survey produced by Victor Hammer, *Oratio De Hominis Dignitate* (1953, no. 52), is one of the few Hammer productions set entirely in roman type: it employs the Emerson font designed by Joseph Blumenthal (like Zapf's Palatino, a modern type not copied from any specific early model) for the main text, with ATF Garamond used for the translation. The strikingly direct and simple title page uses letters reworked by Hammer with a graver to refine the hairlines and serifs to brilliant effect. As with *Feder und Stichel*, the typesetting, presswork, and materials are exceedingly fine but unlike books in the Morris tradition, these eschew decoration and ornament in favor of a more modern aesthetic.

Two books that are close to the private press tradition would be William Everson's (1912–1994) *Novum Psalterium* (1955, no. 55) and Dard Hunter's (1883–1966) *Papermaking by Hand in America* (1950, no. 51). Both were hand set and printed by hand on handmade paper, essentially by one person in total devotion to his craft. They are monumental undertakings (indeed Everson's Psalter was never completed, with only seventy-two pages being printed before he abandoned the project) worthy of the tradition of the great private presses from earlier times. Hunter's book has the distinction of being the first (and only!) book since the invention of printing to have the type designed, cut, and cast by one person, with the same person making the paper by hand, printing the book, and binding it.

Papermaking was a major interest of several other fine presses, including the Bird & Bull Press of Henry Morris and the Perishable Press Limited of Walter Hamady. Hamady's books display exceptional presswork and craftsmanship combined with a nontraditional, whimsical approach, creating volumes that are unlike any others in the field. A large portion of the Perishable Press Limited's (founded 1964) books were printed on paper made by hand by Hamady himself (just as Dard Hunter and Henry Morris made paper for many of their editions). The trials and tribulations of such activity are considered in Hamady's 1982 publication, *Paper Mak-*

ing by Hand (no. 87), set in Palatino and printed on a variety of handmade papers, several of 87 which were manufactured by Hamady himself.

Many presses, such as the Officina Bodoni in Italy, the Rampant Lions and Whittington Presses in England, and in the United States the Windhover, Stone Wall, Adagio, Perishable, Allen, Janus, Arion, Cummington, and Gehenna presses, follow in the private press tradition in at least one respect: they all have a single proprietor who chooses what will be printed and directly oversees every aspect of production, in a way quite like the Kelmscott, Ashendene, and Doves presses. However, all these presses, while steeped in the traditions of fine printing, strive to create books that are of their time.

The British private presses accounted for about a quarter of the pre-1949 selections in this exhibition. Since 1949 the private press tradition has remained strong in England, with the Rampant Lions and Whittington presses each producing marvelous privately printed editions, though their books cannot be considered old-fashioned. Whittington's work in printing elegant volumes, often devoted to various aspects of the history of modern printing, is displayed in two publications: their comprehensive bibliography of an exceptional fine press – *The Stanbrook Abbey Press* (1992, no. 98), typeset in Jan van Krimpen's Romulus font (appropriately enough, considering 98 Stanbrook Abbey's extensive use of Van Krimpen's types); and the sumptuous Whittington Press *Bibliography*, set in their beloved Caslon. To this should be added mention of their publications in other fields, including an exceptional range of books with original wood engravings by such accomplished artists as Miriam MacGregor, Howard Phipps, John O'Connor, and Helmut Weissenborn (all included in the 1982 bibliography of the press, no. 88) and their bibliophilic review 88 *Matrix*, a substantial annual continuously published since 1981.

While exceptional presswork and fine taste in typography have been their hallmark, the books selected to represent the Rampant Lions Press – managed by the father and son team of Will (1912–2001) and Sebastian (b. 1941) Carter – are close to the tradition of artists' books. *Weeds and Wildflowers* with wood engravings by George Mackley (1965, no. 69) and *Cupid and Psyche* (no. 69, 80 80), which printed for the first time woodcuts made (but never published) a century earlier by William Morris and Edward Burne-Jones, both display the fine typography and presswork that is characteristic of this important press from Cambridge, England. Also in the category of books in which illustration plays a major role are the Janus Press edition of *The Circus of Dr. Lao* (1984, no. 93), and Bauersche Giesserei's publication, *Am Wegesrand* (1961, no. 63, with Fritz Kredel's 93, 63 hand-colored woodcuts handsomely set off by George Salter's calligraphy). This is one of the few books included in the exhibition that crossed continents in its production: Kredel (1900–1973) and Salter (1897–1967) were both Germans, refugees from Hitler living in New York. Their beautiful collaboration of woodcut and calligraphy was printed in Frankfurt, Germany.

Several book artists worked on projects for the Overbrook Press in Stamford, Connecticut, which was founded in 1934 by Frank Altschul, an investment banker with a taste for fine books. But the Overbrook Press was not a mere after-hours hobby; it was a substantial operation with full-time employees, including the talented Margaret B. Evans as designer and manager. Among the artists and typographers who worked with the press were Rudolph Ruzicka, W. A. Dwiggins, Bruce Rogers, and Thomas Maitland Cleland (1880–1964), who spent years on the multicol-

58 ored screen prints that illustrate the Overbrook edition of *Manon Lescaut* (1958, no. 58).

With all the technological advances of the last half of the century it is impressive to consider two relatively recent large folio volumes that were entirely set by hand from metal foundry type:

73 Stanley Morison's *John Fell* (1967, no. 73) containing 278 folio pages set, appropriately enough, in the Fell fonts at the Oxford University Press, and Enschedé's *Typefoundries in the Netherlands* – originally scheduled for publication in 1928 by William Edwin Rudge, but not published until

82 1978 – (no. 82) with almost five-hundred folio pages handset in Jan van Krimpen's beautiful Romanée type. Both are remarkable achievements considering the advance of machine composition and alternative typesetting and printing methods in the latter part of the century. More recently, Ian Mortimer at I. M. Imprimit in London, England, has printed on the handpress a large portfolio of elaborate Victorian woodcut initials from the historical collection of the St. Bride

99 Printing Library (1993, no. 99). Still, it is a pleasure to contemplate such beautiful small books
60 as John Fass's *The Alphabet in Various Arrangements* (Hammer Creek Press, 1958, no. 60) with its charming typographic compositions using a surprisingly small number of types, Marvell's *The*

75 *Garden* (no. 75) printed at the press of David R. Godine in Cancelleresca Bastarda type with Lance Hidy's enchanting etchings, *The Presses of the Pacific Islands* printed by the Plantin Press

72 in 1967 (no. 72), or the diminutive *Aschaffenburg* volume designed by Hermann Zapf.

The career of the great type designer/calligrapher/typographer Hermann Zapf has spanned the last half of the century, from hand-set foundry metal type through photo-composition and digital type printed by offset lithography. Indeed, the very first type designed specifically for digital typesetting, Marconi (manufactured for Dr. Ing. Rudolf Hell GmbH in 1976), was designed by Zapf. Zapf's first several dozen alphabet designs, first produced in metal, have had an enormous impact on typography right up to the present day. His design work has always shown exceptional attention to detail, standard of execution, and freshness in design; whether it be letterpress printed hand-set metal type, such as in the *Manuale Typographicum* (his *tour de force*

53 display of typefaces from the D. Stempel AG, 1954, no. 53), or machine-set Linotype with offset
64 printed illustrations as in *Aschaffenburg* (printed by Ludwig Oehms in 1962, no. 64). *Aschaffenburg* is one of the earliest titles in a series of approximately forty books on German localities printed over the past four decades for the bookseller Hermann Emig in Amorbach. The most recent titles in the series have been set digitally and printed by offset lithography.

Also associated with the Stempel Typefoundry was Gotthard de Beauclair (1902–1992), the prolific German book designer. Much of de Beauclair's exceptionally fine design work was done anonymously for Insel Verlag, but he also designed special editions under three imprints: Verlag Ars Librorum, Editions de Beauclair, and the Trajanus Presse. For the latter imprint the books, were printed at the house printing office of Stempel. In addition de Beauclair produced many fine editions for other German publishers, such as Propylaen Verlag and the Maximilian Gesellschaft. Two of his Trajanus Presse books have been selected for inclusion in this cata-

logue: *Tristan und Isolde* (1966, no. 71), the first book printed in Jan Tschichold's Sabon type, 71
with charming hand-colored woodcuts by Fritz Kredel; and the purely typographic *Das Evan-*
gelium Johannes (no. 61), set in Hermann Zapf's Aldus roman and Heraklit Greek types. 61

Even the work of a printer like Giovanni Mardersteig, so famous for his sumptuous hand-press printing, shows the inevitable influence of technological change. Mardersteig's handpress operation, the Officina Bodoni, was founded in 1926; but after World War II Mardersteig said he recognized that the days were gone when he could earn a living for himself and his family exclusively by operating a hand-press."

Fortunately his Officina Bodoni was to thrive side by side with a machine-press facility set up in 1948 (the Stamperia Valdonega.) The argument can even be made – considering such impressive books as *De Divina Proportione* (1956, no. 56), *Alphabetum Romanum* (1960, no. 62), and *The* 56
Fables of Aesop (1973, no. 78) – that the best work of the Officina Bodoni came after the war, de- 62, 78
spite Mardersteig's attention being divided between the hand press and machine operation. The small machine typesetting (exclusively by Monotype) and machine-printing operation was established after the war, based on the principles of careful composition and exceptional presswork that prevailed at the Officina Bodoni. It was there at the Stamperia Valdonega that Mardersteig printed his lovely edition of Ovid's *Metamorphoses* (1958, no. 59) for the Limited 59
Editions Club in New York. It is an austerely elegant book, with Hans Erni's simple yet expressive line etchings highlighting the classical, straightforward typography in Bruce Rogers's Centaur type. Giovanni Mardersteig's son, Martino, continues his father's respect for traditional values in fine bookmaking while expanding the operation further into high-quality offset lithography, and computer typesetting from fonts specially digitized for the exclusive use of the Stamperia Valdonega. Shown here is *Lo Splendore della Verona affrescata* (1983, no. 91) combining 91
superlative letterpress printing (from Giovanni Mardersteig's Dante type, set by Monotype) and exceptionally fine color offset illustrations.

The French, of course, are best known for their contribution to the field of *livres d'artiste*, many of which were printed pre-1949 and covered in Hutner's essay. America has, however, made significant contributions in this area, as chronicled by Elizabeth Phillips and Tony Zwicker in their *American Livre de Peintre* exhibition, held also at the Grolier Club.

A wide variety of printing techniques – from hand-pulled intaglio etching and lithography to silk screen and computer-plotted drawing – were employed by fifteen different artists to interpret the words of the Persian mystic poet Rumi in Vincent FitzGerald & Company's edition of the *Divan-E-Shams*, mentioned earlier on page xx. The text has been printed by the traditional letterpress method, but using photo-polymer plates of computer-set type.

Perhaps the artist most attuned to the historical aspects of artists' books was Leonard Baskin (1922–2000), who produced a sustained and substantial body of work at his Gehenna Press while pursuing a career as a fine artist. Baskin's artwork is included in collections as diverse as the Vatican in Rome and the Museum of Modern Art in New York. The books printed at his Gehenna Press most often contain his own prints – as is the case with the monumental *Icones Librorum*

96   *Artifices* (1988, no. 96) with Baskin's fantastic etchings. Occasionally, however, he utilized the
70   work of other artists or purely typographic material, such as in his *Flosculi Sententiarum* (1967,
      no. 70) wonderfully printed by Harold McGrath from printer's ornaments that had once be-
      longed to Bruce Rogers, with the text set in Centaur on a stock of beautiful handmade paper. In
      these and many other editions the breadth of Baskin's knowledge of the history of printmak-
      ing and fine editions, along with the artist's keen sense of proportion, contribute to an impor-
      tant body of work. Colin Franklin, author of *The Private Press*, has described the Gehenna Press
      as "a private press whose long history includes exquisite small etchings, wild monotypes and
      expressionist woodcuts, delicate experiments with fleurons and shaped typography, colour-
      printing, art history, social conscience and an impressive list of new poetry, all in a context of
      scholarly recollection, [which] must one day be seen to rest near the summit of them all."

      Andrew Hoyem (b. 1935) at his Arion Press has produced special editions in collaboration
83   with several eminent artists. *Moby-Dick* (1979, no. 83) with wood engravings by Barry Moser, a
86   student of Baskin's, and *Apocalypse* (1982, no. 86) with woodcuts by Jim Dine, are two of the
      most successful Arion Press publications.

      Moser was proprietor of his own press in the Baskin/Gehenna tradition: the Pennyroyal
      Press, where Baskin's former pressman, Harold McGrath, printed fine editions containing
      Moser's illustrations. Moser's dark, precise style seems well suited to Mary Shelley's *Franken-
      stein*, which the press issued in a limited edition of 350 copies printed from Poliphilus and Wil-
92   helm Klingsporschrift types on specially made Strathmore paper in 1983 (no. 92).

      Hoyem hails from California, which has had an unusually high concentration of fine print-
      ing activity. It was in San Francisco that Adrian Wilson (1923–1988) settled after being incarcer-
      ated as a conscientious objector during World War II (he spent time in a camp with another
      printer included in this catalogue, William Everson). Wilson's wonderfully playful *Printing for
57   Theater* (1957, no. 57) and Everson's sumptuous essay in the great tradition of the private presses
55   – *Novum Psalterium* (mentioned above, no. 55) – are two books indicative of some of the activi-
      ty in the Bay area.

84   In 1981 the Allen Press of Greenbrae, California, printed a handsome bibliography (no. 84)
      documenting their work on forty-five publications. The press was started as a part-time opera-
      tion, but was operated full time by Dorothy and Lewis Allen from 1950 until just a few years
      ago. Their first nine books were printed by hand feeding paper on a power-driven platen press,
      but after that each book was entirely printed by hand on dampened handmade paper, in the tra-
      dition of the great private presses – one of the very few operations printing exclusively on a
      handpress after the World War II. Also challenging the march of technology by printing entire-
      ly by hand was the Plain Wrapper Press of Gabriel Rummonds and Alessandro Zanella. Rum-
      monds began printing on a modest scale in Ecuador, and later for a brief time in New York City,
      but his work blossomed in Verona, Italy, where he printed some outstanding books, the most
79   impressive of which is probably *Seven Saxon Poems* translated by Jorge Luis Borges (1974, no. 79)
      with blind-embossed images and cover relief by the sculptor by Arnaldo Pomodoro.

      Included in the California group are two books printed in Los Angeles by Saul (1905–1984) and

Lillian Marks's Plantin Press, one an exhibition catalogue and the other a privately printed edition: *A Descriptive Catalogue of the Book of Common Prayer* (1955, no. 54) and *Presses of the Pacific Islands* (published by the Plantin Press in 1967, no. 72). After emigrating to the United States from Warsaw, Poland, in 1928 Saul Marks founded the press with his wife, Lillian (whom he married in 1928). Marks arranged the typography and decorative type ornaments with great agility and originality. The Plantin Press is an example of how "commercial" printing can aspire to the level of a fine press, a possibility Updike and Meynell had demonstrated earlier in the century. One of the finest examples of this dual role would be Joseph Blumenthal's (1897–1990) Spiral Press in New York City, also represented – like the Plantin Press – by an exceptionally handsome exhibition catalogue, *Chinese Calligraphy and Painting in the Collection of John M. Crawford, Jr.* (1962, no. 65), and by a privately printed edition, *Ecclesiastes*, with drawings by Ben Shahn engraved on wood by Stefan Martin (published by the Spiral Press in 1965, no. 68). 54 72 65 68

Lest one think all the activity in America was concentrated on the two coasts, there has been a plethora of activity in the Midwest. Cherryburn, Cummington, Prairie Press, Stone Wall, and Windhover, among many other presses, have made a significant contribution to postwar fine bookmaking in the United States.

R. Hunter Middleton (1898–1992), a type designer for the Ludlow Corporation by profession, private press printer by avocation, showed exceptional skill in the printing of wood engravings in his portfolio of Thomas Bewick's prints (1970, no. 76) produced at his Cherryburn Press in Chicago. By expending microscopic care on each subject, sometimes spending several hours on makeready for a single cut, he was able to bring out the inherent beauty of the woodcuts to a degree not seen even in Bewick's time. 76

Another impressive undertaking for a part-time printer is the Adagio Press's *C-S The Master Craftsman* (1969, no, 74). Leonard Bahr (1934–1992), proprietor of the Adagio Press, worked in advertising during the day, spending evenings and weekends hand setting type and printing on a Chandler & Price platen press. Meticulous composition, most often using unusual European typefaces, and superior presswork characterize the work of the press. Most of the output was small in format, but *C-S The Master Craftsman* is a splendid exception, being folio in format to accommodate a leaf from the monumental Doves Press *Bible* (see no. 4), elucidated with texts by John Dreyfus and Norman H. Strouse. Bahr's modest colophon gives a hint of the effort involved in producing such a substantial book in off-hours on relatively small equipment: "All in all, this has been a somewhat ambitious project for a spare time press. It has taken about a year of planning and work to get this far, and there remains enough work to fill several more months. It is my hope that, relative to the problems involved, you will consider the result at least satisfactory." The end result is a fitting tribute to its contents, printed from hand-set Palatino and Pascal types on handmade Tovill paper; hand bound by Fritz and Trudi Eberhardt in quarter vellum with marbled paper sides. 74 4

Kim Merker (b. 1932) is the proprietor of the Stone Wall Press where he has demonstrated great dexterity in combining papers (Rives and Mulberry), typefaces (Romanée and Open Kapitalen), and illustrations (semiabstract wood engravings by John Roy) in Theodore Roethke's *Sequence,*

67   *Sometimes Metaphysical* (1963, no. 67). He later set up the Windhover Press "primarily for the preservation and dissemination of those skills that go into creating the hand-produced book," printing W. S. Merwin's *Robert the Devil* under that imprint in 1981 with far different illustrations (wood engravings in a somewhat retrospective style by Roxanne Sexauer) and typography (Dante, Bembo italic, and Centaur types on specially made Windhover paper), yet still with har-

85   monious and innovative results (no. 85). For yet a third imprint, the Iowa Center for the Book, Merker printed a special deluxe edition of Samuel Beckett's *Company* with thirteen etchings by

89   Dellas Henke (1983, no. 89), set in Jan van Krimpen's Spectrum type and printed on Arches paper.

      Merker's bibliographer, Sidney Berger, has aptly called Merker "a master of his trade." The same can surely be said of Merker's teacher, Harry Duncan (1916 – 1997). Starting out in 1941 in Cummington, Massachusetts (at the Cummington School of Arts, hence the name "Cummington Press"), with the support of the director Kathleen Frazier, moving from there to Iowa in 1956 and then to Omaha, Nebraska, Duncan printed and published fine editions of excep-

97   tional writers over the course of four decades. His 1989 edition of the *Poems of Catullus* (no. 97) shows his mastery in the arrangement of pure typography, utilizing two of the relatively uncommon fonts in his repertoire: Eric Gill's Joanna for the text paired with Jan van Krimpen's Romulus Open type for the initials and display setting. Both Merker's and Duncan's books are eminently readable, showing great respect and sensitivity to the author's words, but always demonstrating fresh and new approaches that build on the traditions of the typographic book while breaking some barriers along the way.

★   ★   ★

Daniel Berkeley Updike concluded his monumental study of printing types (1922) by saying that "in every period there have been better or worse types employed in better or worse ways. The better types employed in better ways have been used by the educated printer acquainted with standards and history, directed by taste and a sense of fitness of things, and facing the industrial conditions and the needs of his time. Such men have made of printing an art. . . . The outlook for typography is as good as ever it was – and much the same. Its future depends largely on the knowledge and taste of educated men." A similar sentiment was echoed more than half a century later by Joseph Blumenthal, who ended his survey of *The Printed Book in America* (1977) with the observation that the "art of the book, one of the slender graces of civilization, works its charms on each new generation." Both Updike and Blumenthal themselves produced work to the highest standards, and have been included more than once in this retrospective of the art of printing in the twentieth century.

      This catalogue is intended to give a glimpse of how the generations of the past century have displayed knowledge and taste in raising printing to an art. The twentieth century has seen its share of turmoil and upheaval – but also great advances and accomplishments. The arts, including the art of the book, have seen a greater profusion and diversity than perhaps at any other time in the history of mankind. Yet there is no reason to think that time will stand still, and that advancement will cease. One can be sure that new and valid expressions will continue to develop, and that a superb exhibition of books of the century could be held in the year 2099, despite the progress of digital imaging, computer driven typesetting, and other media. We trust that the one hundred books exhibited here will compare favorably with those that future centuries will offer, as we feel they do with the significant accomplishments of centuries past.

Jerry Kelly

NOTES ON A CENTURY FOR THE CENTURY

1. L'Imprimerie Nationale (Pierre Bonnard); Paris, France, 1900
PAUL VERLAINE · PARALLÈLEMENT

What makes *Parallèlement* so interesting – apart from its considerable aesthetic merit – is that for a book of over one hundred years ago, it appears astonishingly modern. Only a few years before, the Kelmscott Press, for example, was producing superb Arts and Crafts books that were completely antiquarian in appearance.

In Paris, the art dealer Ambroise Vollard, had the idea that France's greatest painters should illustrate books with original artwork. At his insistence, what we consider the modern *livre d'artiste* was born. *Parallèlement* was the first of his books, and remains to this day an outstanding example of the genre.

Inspired by the modernity of Verlaine's text, Pierre Bonnard (1867–1947) produced more than one hundred lithographs that were printed in rose-sanguine ink, along with nine wood engravings in black. The text was printed separately at the Imprimerie Nationale in a new font, Garamond italic, based on a type designed in 1540. The text, sometimes asymmetrically arranged, achieves a harmony with the sensuous illustrations. The meshing of words and image weaves a black and rose tapestry unique for its time.

2. Theodore Low De Vinne; New York, New York, 1901
T. L. DE VINNE · TITLE-PAGES AS SEEN BY A PRINTER

Theodore Low De Vinne (1828–1914) and his press dominated most of the fine and commercial printing in America in the last quarter of the nineteenth century. In 1884 he became one of the founders of the Grolier Club, and his press printed the club's first publication, *A Decree of Star Chamber.*

All of De Vinne's work was produced with precision and care; the presswork was always immaculate, if a little unimaginative in design. Yet occasionally, De Vinne's sense of scholarship and design did merge to achieve distinctive harmony, as here in his *Title-Pages,* printed for the Grolier Club in 1901. The book contains a short history of printing, with an analysis of flowers, rules, black-letter and roman type, and composition. Superbly printed on handmade paper, these facsimiles of title pages from the early days of printing to the present show De Vinne at his best.

3. Ashendene Press (C. H. St. John Hornby); Chelsea, England, 1902
DANTE ALIGHIERI · LO INFERNO

C.H. St. John Hornby (1867–1946), a successful managing director of a large British book distributor, founded his Ashendene Press in 1894, influenced – as were so many of his colleagues – by William Morris and his Kelmscott Press. And like Morris, he found his inspiration in the past, which in Hornby's instance was the Renaissance rather than the Middle Ages. Hornby possessed the means to secure the best printers, the best illustrators, the best materials, and not least, his own proprietary typeface, Subiaco, as well as others. Under Hornby's direction, the press flourished until 1935, a long and distinguished career for any private press.

Like the rest of the three-volume *Divine Comedy, Lo Inferno* is superbly printed in black, red, and gold, with red and green flourishes hand drawn by the calligrapher Graily Hewitt. It contains fifteen woodcuts by Charles Keats, from drawings by R. Catterson Smith, and more than thirty decorative initials by Smith.

4. Doves Press (T. J. Cobden-Sanderson); Hammersmith, England, 1903–1905

THE ENGLISH BIBLE

One of the best-known British press books is the five-volume *Bible,* printed over several years by the Doves Press, which was founded by T. J. Cobden-Sanderson (1840–1922) in 1900. With the aid of the ubiquitous and influential Emery Walker as partner, a house proprietary type was designed based on a Nicolaus Jensen original from fifteenth-century Venice. For sixteen years the press flourished, producing books of pure typographic beauty. *The English Bible* is famous for its opening page, with a magisterial "I" designed by the great English calligrapher Edward Johnston. This Bible has no illustrations, relying entirely on the beauty of the type and its superb imposition on fine handmade paper for its powerful effect.

5. The Eragny Press (Lucien & Esther Pissarro); Hammersmith, England, 1906

BEN JONSON · SONGS BY BEN JONSON

Lucien Pissarro (1863–1944) was the eldest son of the Impressionist painter Camille Pissarro. In 1883 he moved from Paris to London to live with an uncle, ostensibly to improve his English. After marrying, Pissarro searched about for a career in the arts, despite his mother's objection to his following in his father's footsteps as an artist. He was much influenced by the Neo-Impressionists, particularly Seurat, and by English Arts and Crafts publications, especially those of William Morris. He entered the circle around Charles Ricketts and Charles Shannon, proprietors of the Vale Press. This association fueled Lucien's love of bookmaking and book illustration and ultimately led to the founding, in 1894, of the Eragny Press (named for the family's home village in France). From 1896 until 1903, Pissarro's work was printed using Ricketts' Vale type. By 1903, Lucien had designed his own type, Brook, and his last sixteen books were published using an alphabet Colin Franklin has called "the most beautiful font invented in [that] period."

The woodcuts were designed and cut by Lucien, and printed by him and his wife, Esther, in a palette of rich reds, greens, yellows, and purples. This, together with the type, make the last books of the press some of the most beautiful and distinctive of the early twentieth century.

6. Doves Press (T. J. Cobden-Sanderson); Hammersmith, England, 1908

ROBERT BROWNING · MEN & WOMEN

Another splendid example of Doves Press printing is the two-volume rendition of Robert Browning's *Men & Women.* Once again the chief beauty of the work is the simply composed and superbly printed text on beautiful paper. Here, calligraphic flourishes in blue and green, hand drawn by Edward Johnston in some sets, enhance the page. Twelve copies were printed on vellum.

The partnership with Emery Walker eventually soured. Cobden-Sanderson had become increasingly proprietary about the press and increasingly resentful of Walker, without whom, it must be said, he probably would not have succeeded at all. Cobden-Sanderson closed the press down in December of 1916 and issued the final edition of the *Catalogue Raisonné.*

Then followed one of the more bizarre and dramatic episodes in printing history. In 1917 Cobden-Sanderson threw the Doves type, matrices, etc., from Hammersmith Bridge into the Thames River. He had printed a "Consecratio" to commemorate the event, which ends, "May the River, with its tides and flow, pass over them to and from the great sea for ever and ever and pass from change to change upon the Tides of Time, untouched by other use." By that he probably meant Emery Walker, who, as partner in the press, properly and legally owned half the right to the types.

7. The Riverside Press (Bruce Rogers); Cambridge, Massachusetts, 1909

AUGUST BERNARD · GEOFROY TORY

Bruce Rogers (1870–1957), an artist and designer from Indiana, was to become one of the most distinguished and revered American book designers and typographers. Rogers came to work at Houghton Mifflin's Riverside Press in 1896, shortly after the departure of D. B. Updike. While there, he designed August Bernard's work on Geofroy Tory, the great French engineer and fine Royal Printer under François I. Rogers reengraved Tory's original designs, which, with a few exceptions, are rendered in their original size. This reinterpretive ability was one of Rogers's hallmarks, as is his trademark thistle which appears on the title-page. Though Rogers was to have a long career ending only with death in 1957, the *Geofroy Tory* is one of his early masterpieces, showing his mastery of allusive typography, design, and illustration.

8. Thomas Bird Mosher; Portland, Maine, 1913

EDWARD CALVERT · TEN SPIRITUAL DESIGNS

In many ways, Thomas Bird Mosher (1852–1923) stands alone in the history of American printing and publishing. In Joseph Blumenthal's estimation, "He is the first American to have established and sustained a program, over thirty-two years (1891–1923), of splendid literary output in consistently felicitous typographic form."

Mosher's books were usually small in size and printed in very limited editions. Edward Calvert's *Designs,* from copper, wood, and stone originals, is an example of Mosher's work at its best. Although he consistently used the finest materials and obtained outstanding presswork, there is something very American about almost all of Mosher's output, in its four-square simplicity and directness.

It is true that, in the years before copyright, publishers like Mosher routinely reproduced work without making authorial compensation – a practice that earned him the sobriquet of the "Passionate Pirate of Portland." Yet Mosher also performed a very real literary as well as aesthetic service, providing well-produced and well-edited texts to bibliophiles in the first part of the century.

9. The Merrymount Press (Daniel Berkeley Updike); Boston, Massachusetts, 1917

WALTER PRICHARD EATON · NEWARK
Wood engravings by Rudolph Ruzicka

From the very beginning of the Merrymount Press in 1893, Daniel Berkeley Updike (1860–1941), who had initially entered printing reluctantly and by chance, hired artists and type designers from America and England. Among them were figures such as T. M. Cleland, W. A. Dwiggins, Bertram Grosvenor Goodhue, Richard Anning Bell, and Herbert Horne, all of whom went on to distinguished careers.

One of Updike's happiest affiliations was with the artist Rudolph Ruzicka (1883–1978), who had emigrated from his native Bohemia to New York. Temperamentally and aesthetically well suited to each other, they formed a lifelong friendship and professional association. Several of the great books of the press were beautifully illustrated with engravings by Ruzicka.

In the instance of *Newark,* done for the Carteret Book Club, the wood engravings, five of them full page, form the *raison d'être* for the enterprise and are among the most powerful and elegant of any he made. Updike's superb use of Caslon for the title page and the setting of the text by Walter Prichard Eaton combine to make this volume one of the press's finest from the second decade of the century.

10. The Merrymount Press (Daniel Berkeley Updike); Boston, Massachusetts, 1921

WASHINGTON IRVING · NOTES AND JOURNAL OF TRAVEL IN EUROPE

Aquatints by Rudolph Ruzicka

In 1921 the Grolier Club approached D. B. Updike (who was to become an honorary member in 1926) to design an edition of Washington Irving's European *Notes*. Once again Updike chose Rudolph Ruzicka (also a Grolierite and eventual honorary member) to furnish the illustrations. These illustrations were executed in aquatint and highlighted with details picked out in watercolor.

In his recollections, Ruzicka wrote about the making of the illustrations, his first use of aquatint: "I did a decorative title-page for the set, as well as an aquatint illustration for each of the three volumes. But that was the first time that I had tried aquatint, and I sweated over it. I colored all the illustrations myself, every one of them. I was very proud of the results at the time, and it's actually rather a gem."

11. Bremer Presse; Munich, Germany, 1921

DANTE ALIGHIERI · LA DIVINA COMMEDIA

Germany's Bremer Presse was founded in 1911 by Willy Wiegand (1884–1961). Wiegand, the son of a successful industrialist, possessed the means and the taste to underwrite the ambitious productions of the press until it ceased operation in 1939 on the eve of World War II.

Each of this press's books, such as the magnificent edition of Dante's *La Divina Commedia*, depended for effect on the beauty of the type and the expert printing on handmade paper. The only decoration the press ever used were initial letters, in this case (as in most of its books) by the very talented Anna Simons, a student of Edward Johnston. The felicitous balance of Simons's initials and Wiegand's roman type demonstrates the sheer simplicity and beauty of a Bremer Presse page.

12. Bremer Presse; Munich, Germany, 1923–1924

HOMER · ILIAD AND ODYSSEY

Willy Wiegand designed a distinctive Greek type for his Bremer Presse publication of Homer's *Iliad* and *Odyssey*. The type has a degree of movement, letter strokes tilting left and right so that one almost senses a scribal hand. The end margins are generous, and the line count, slightly indented below each block of text, acts as a visual tab for moving on to the next page.

Impeccably printed on a beautiful cream Zanders handmade paper, page after page of Homer's epic sweeps along in majestic procession, enabling even those unable to read the language to sense its narrative flow. The timelessness and simplicity of design are classic.

13. Officina Bodoni (Giovanni Mardersteig); Montagnola di Lugano, Switzerland, 1924

JOHANN WOLFGANG VON GOETHE · DAS ROEMISCHE CARNEVAL 1788

Giovanni Mardersteig (1892–1977) was German by birth, growing up in Weimar in a house where members of the art community met, notably Count Harry Kessler of the Cranach Presse. Guided by a family which included well-known artists, Mardersteig's education was directed toward art and literature.

In 1916 he left Germany for Switzerland because of ill health. Later he became an editor involved in book production with the noted Munich publisher Kurt Wolff. In 1922, Mardersteig purchased a handpress and obtained permission from the Italian government to cast new type from the original matrices of the great Italian printer Bodoni, after whom he named his press, and a commission to print the complete works of Italy's most celebrated contemporary author, Gabriele d'Annunzio.

Two years later, Mardersteig printed Goethe's *Das Roemische Carneval* in the Bodoni italic type that flows across the page with gusto and spirit. There is only one touch of color, the red of the press's own mark. The text is the original German of 1788. The edition was exquisitely printed in an edition of 224 copies on Fabriano handmade paper, with six copies on vellum.

14. Bremer Presse; Munich, Germany, 1925

S. AURELII AUGUSTINI · DE CIVITATE DEI

In 1925, the Bremer Presse issued Saint Augustine's monumental *De Civitate Dei* (*The City of God*). With its initials by Anna Simons, the powerful title page is among the most beautiful produced by the press. Joseph Blumenthal's apt characterization of Bremer Presse books is nowhere more apposite than for the Augustine: "The books were clearly made to glorify the written word and the traditional art of the book, which they do with great distinction."

Wiegand's small, clear roman type, set very tightly, is used here with great impact, matching the power of Saint Augustine's words. The specifics of type, inking, presswork, and paper are close to perfection. Much of the press's production exhibits a design philosophy shared by certain English presses, most notably the Doves Press.

15. Cranach Presse; Weimar, Germany, 1926

VIRGIL · THE ECLOGUES OF VIRGIL

Woodcuts by Aristide Maillol

The Cranach Presse, one of the great German presses of the first half of this century, was founded by Count Harry Kessler (1868–1937) in Weimar.

The first of a triumvirate of Cranach masterpieces in this exhibition is the *Eclogues of Virgil,* in a translation by J. H. Mason. The book is printed in a roman type designed by Edward Prince under the direction of Emery Walker, to whom the book is generously dedicated, with an italic type by Edward Johnston, and a title-page and initials cut by Eric Gill. The true glory of the book, however, lies in the forty-four wood engravings and additional decorated initials and ornaments by the French artist Aristide Maillol (1861–1944), and is the first of many books illustrated by the great sculptor.

The book is printed on handmade paper specially produced near Paris by Maillol's nephew. There were three separate editions: German, English and French, making the *Eclogues* an international enterprise in every respect. The English edition comprised 225 copies on handmade paper, thirty-five on Imperial Japanese paper, and six on vellum. With the clarity and classic simplicity of the woodcuts juxtaposed and perfectly balanced with the weight and beauty of the type, the *Eclogues* is a monument of twentieth-century printing.

16. Gebr. Klingspor (Rudolf Koch); Offenbach am Main, Germany, 1926

DIE VIER EVANGELIEN

Rudolf Koch (1876–1934) was known in the first half of the twentieth century as one of Germany's most proficient calligraphers and designers. In 1926, while working at the Klingspor type foundry in Offenbach-am-Main, he first used his Bible Gothic typeface (later dubbed Peter Jessen-Schrift) in *Die Vier Evangelien (The Four Gospels),* an edition that he privately subsidized. While clearly in the tradition of the German gothic blackletter, Koch's version differs from the usual prototypes in being far easier to read.

17. "The Sign of the Dolphin" (George W. Jones); London, England, 1929

A DISTINGUISHED FAMILY OF FRENCH PRINTERS OF THE SIXTEENTH CENTURY: HENRI AND ROBERT ESTIENNE

George W. Jones (1860–1942) opened his printing establishment at the Sign of the Dolphin, in St. Bride Lane, when he came to London in 1889. He advertised himself as a "Superior Printer." Born in Upton-on-Severn, Jones had served his printing apprenticeship in the city of Worcester and was later employed at the Darien Press in Edinburgh, where he taught the typographic arts. He continued his teaching in London.

Jones was an enthusiastic collector of early typography, and he was ultimately to design his own type, Granjon, which was first used to illustrate his book on Robert Granjon (a virtual twin, in style, to the book exhibited here). In this book Jones employed his new type, Estienne, which had been designed for the Mergenthaler Linotype Company. Although Jones did all sorts of job printing, such as menus and calling cards, he was also capable of designing books of great typographic beauty. His use of type and typographic ornament in his Granjon and Estienne studies demonstrate his knowledge of period printing. The design, the printing on Kelmscott handmade paper, and the vellum and decorated paper binding are all exemplary.

18. John Henry Nash; San Francisco, California, 1929

DANTE ALIGHIERI · THE DIVINE COMEDY

John Henry Nash (1871–1947) was born in Canada, where he learned to be a type compositor. He settled in San Francisco in 1895 and for the next twenty-one years worked in a number of the city's printing establishments. In 1916, at the age of forty-five, he set up his own printing office, became one of the founders of the Book Club of California, and printed many of the club's early books.

In 1923 Nash began what is generally considered his finest work, the four-volume *Divine Comedy* of Dante. Nash said that he strove to make this presentation a monument to Dante, to his translator (Melville Anderson), and to the printing art. He knew this was to be his masterpiece. The pages are set in Cloister Light Face, with printed green columnar rules, recalling the rules drawn in early manuscripts by scribes.

19. The Pynson Printers (Elmer Adler); New York, New York, 1929

ALFRED E. HAMILL (Introduction) · THE DECORATIVE WORK OF T. M. CLELAND

Elmer Adler (1884–1961) came to printing after an early career as advertising manager of his family's Rochester, New York, clothing business. In 1922, possessing both the means and the desire, he set up his own printing establishment in New York City, naming it the Pynson Printers, after the early English Huguenot printer, Richard Pynson. The press was committed to the printing of fine work, and for eighteen years turned out books and ephemera that were – and are – highly prized and avidly collected. Adler went on to found *The Colophon,* a magazine devoted to the book arts, for which he served as publisher, editor, and printer. In the 1920s he formed an association with Random House.

In 1929, Adler published by himself a book celebrating the work of the distinguished typographer and highly prolific designer, Thomas Maitland Cleland. Cleland had, in his early career, done work for D. B. Updike's Merrymount Press and for the Bruce Type Foundry as well as producing designs for the business industry, including catalogues, promotional literature, Christmas cards, and calendars. All this work received the same care, attention, and imagination he brought to his book design. Some of his best work is celebrated in this quarto volume, which was in planning and production for five years.

20. Druck der Mainzer Presse (Rudolf Koch & Fritz Kredel); Mainz, Germany, 1929–1930

RUDOLF KOCH · DAS BLUMENBUCH

Das Blumenbuch (*Book of Flowers*) represents in all its facets the *ne plus ultra* of illustrated book design. The genesis of the book rests in a trip Koch took in Germany with his young children to gather wildflowers. Koch, who began to make drawings of them, then decided to reproduce them in a book. For this project Koch enlisted his friend Fritz Kredel, himself a fine artist and designer, to make woodcuts from his drawings. This was done over a period of years. Koch wrote, "This is how my collection of 250 different flowers came into being – collected at random – I sketched the ones which grew in and around Offenbach. This collection is intended to give people a taste of summer while in winter." In the original edition, each woodcut was printed on a separate sheet, hand colored, and collected in fascicles.

21. Cranach Presse; Weimar, Germany, 1929–1930

WILLIAM SHAKESPEARE · THE TRAGEDIE OF HAMLET
Woodcuts by Edward Gordon Craig

In 1929–30 the Cranach Presse issued its monumental *Hamlet*. The project was reportedly initiated at the inception of the press. Edward Gordon Craig labored for seventeen years on the woodcuts, and the resulting illustrations were among the finest work he ever produced. A seldom-noted detail is that the woodcut on page 169 was given a touch of red hand-coloring.

Gordon Craig announced this project in 1908, intending to publish the book himself in what he called a "Director's Edition." A professional and innovative stage designer, he had planned to write complete notes on every detail of theatrical production – scenery, costumes, lighting, furniture, ground plans of each scene, movements of actors – but could not raise the money for so ambitious a production. Learning of Craig's failed plans, Count Kessler arranged in 1912 to undertake publication. Work was begun, and though the onset of World War I put a temporary halt to it, the project was resumed in 1927.

In this setting of Shakespeare's great tragedy, edited by J. Dover Wilson, Craig's woodcuts are complemented by the fraktur type, designed by Edward Johnston and based on a letter first used by Füst and Schoeffer in their Mainz *Psalter* of 1457. The type was cut by Edward Prince. The textured, handmade paper contributes a tonal mood to the *mise-en-page*.

22. The Lakeside Press; Chicago, Illinois, 1930

HERMAN MELVILLE · MOBY-DICK; OR, THE WHALE
Illustrations by Rockwell Kent

R. R. Donnelley & Sons, hugely successful commercial printers, publishers, and binders, had long dominated the Chicago printing establishment. The Lakeside Press was founded to handle fine printing for the company. Under the design directorship of William A. Kittredge, the Lakeside Press produced notable work for both Chicago's Caxton Club and the Limited Editions Club. Kittredge commissioned a number of the leading artists and designers of the day, such as Rudolph Ruzicka, Edward A. Wilson, and W. A. Dwiggins to provide illustrations, choosing Rockwell Kent to illustrate Herman Melville's *Moby-Dick,* our choice from a series of four splendidly printed literary classics published by the press. The other handsome volumes are *Walden, Two Years before the Mast,* and Poe's *Tales.*

Kent's illustrations for *Moby-Dick,* used as chapter headings, are executed in his distinctive, powerful black-and-white linear style; and they complement the strong Caslon Old Face typography and dramatic decorative initials. The nautical theme is emphasized by the unusual use of harpoon-shaped motifs bracketing the folios.

Melville's classic tale, possessing a decidedly American character, forthright and strong, has often tempted book designers and printers, as we shall see elsewhere in this catalogue.

23. The Grabhorn Press; San Francisco, California, 1930

WALT WHITMAN · LEAVES OF GRASS
Woodcuts by Valenti Angelo

Another of the great American West Coast presses was founded in San Francisco in 1919 by Edwin (1890–1968) and Robert (1900–1973) Grabhorn. Their press was to have a long and distinguished life, lasting until 1965. Edwin, the elder brother, learned the printing business at an uncle's printing shop in Indiana. Later a music publisher in Seattle, he finally settled in San Francisco. After working alone there as a printer for seven years, Edwin was joined by Robert. In 1920, the Book Club of California commissioned the young firm to design a book. By 1923, the brothers were developing a distinctive style of their own, and that year one of their books was among the "Fifty Books of the Year" chosen by the American Institute of Graphic Arts.

By 1930, they had produced shelves of fine printing and were about to create one of their masterpieces, Walt Whitman's *Leaves of Grass*. It was to prove a mammoth undertaking. More than four hundred pages were printed damp in two-page forms on handmade paper, with handsome illustrations by Valenti Angelo, an artist long associtaed with and frequently employed by the Grabhorns for their work. Edwin later described the lengthy trial-and-error process for their design of the Whitman text, down to the "shuddering" of the hand-fed Colts Amory press for each heavy impression. We meet the press again in 1940, with the masterly printing of the first of three press bibliographies (no. 42).

24. Cambridge University Press; Cambridge, England, 1930

STANLEY MORISON · JOHN BELL

Born in Essex, England, Stanley Morison (1889–1967) became an outstanding figure in twentieth-century printing and historical research. By turns a printer, scholar, and book and type designer, he excelled in all three and left a notable body of work in each area. All of these skills and abilities came together in his *John Bell,* published by the Cambridge University Press, where he served as typographic advisor, from January of 1925, initially with its formidable university printer, Walter Lewis, and later with his successor, Brooke Crutchley. He was already acting in the same capacity for the Monotype Corporation which, under his direction, was beginning its program of reissuing classic typefaces.

John Bell (1745–1831), a British publisher of books and newspapers, had produced for his use what have been called the first "modern" types. In this survey of Bell's work, Morison mixed text and illustration, collotypes and alphabets with his characteristic brilliance. The informative text was printed in type newly cast from Bell's original matrices. In this book Morison had immersed himself in Bell's multifaceted world, which went beyond his usual essays on printing and calligraphy. The presswork and the high quality of the color prints and facsimiles, along with Morison's text, make the book a bibliophilic treasure.

25. The Merrymount Press (Daniel Berkeley Updike); Boston, Massachusetts, 1930

THE BOOK OF COMMON PRAYER

In 1928, the Episcopal Church Commission once again revised the *Book of Common Prayer,* and a printing for a new standard version was undertaken under the sponsorship of J. Pierpont Morgan, supervised by his librarian, Belle da Costa Greene. Four presses and designers – the Cambridge and Oxford University Presses, D. B. Updike, and Bruce Rogers – were asked to submit specimen pages. Updike and his Merrymount Press were the ultimate, and probably the irresistible, choices.

Over the next few years the project was to consume Updike, who put his heart and soul into it. Few printers were better equipped than this devout Anglican to handle the project, and the result was magnificent. For Updike it was the culmination of everything he believed in and understood, and every facet of his personality and sensibility was called upon to produce this masterpiece of print and spirit. The specially procured Janson type here assumes a rare majesty. The sober elegance of page after page of superbly printed text, both distinct, appropriate to the liturgy, and eminently readable, makes the work at once fresh and everlasting.

26. The Golden Cockerel Press; Waltham Saint Lawrence, England, 1931

THE FOUR GOSPELS OF LORD JESUS CHRIST
Wood engravings by Eric Gill

The Golden Cockerel Press was founded in 1920 by Harold M. Taylor at Waltham Saint Lawrence. Taylor's original aim had been to publish new works by young authors, in addition to printing fine editions of established work. After several years, illness necessitated Taylor's retirement, and the press was purchased in early 1924 by Robert Gibbings, an illustrator and wood engraver. Gibbings added new equipment, and the press began to go from one critical success to another, issuing works of great interest and beauty.

In 1931, the press issued one of its finest books, largely the work of Eric Gill (1892–1940), the protean artist, sculptor, and typographer. *The Four Gospels* is arguably Gill's greatest achievement in bookmaking and one of the great private press books of the century. Sixty-four wood engravings and initial letters by Gill are printed in dense black and form a powerful complement to the text, handsomely printed in the press's Golden Cockerel type.

27. Joh. Enschedé en Zonen (Jan van Krimpen); Haarlem, The Netherlands, 1931

HOMER · THE ILIAD AND THE ODYSSEY

Jan van Krimpen (1892–1958) was born in Gouda, Holland, and studied at the Academy of Art in the Hague, leaving at the age of twenty. At school he became interested in lettering and calligraphy and began to immerse himself in these disciplines. In 1923, he began working for the venerable typefounding firm of Joh. Enschedé in Haarlem. His first type, finished in 1925, was Lutetia, cut by P. H. Rädisch, a distinguished Leipzig-trained punchcutter.

In 1931, the Limited Editions Club published Alexander Pope's translation of Homer's epics. The two volumes constituted one of van Krimpen's early great works, printed in one of his most beautiful types, Romanée. Of these books, and of this type, the British book scholar John Dreyfus wrote, "The text of Pope's translation was done the fullest justice by a spacious setting in Romanée. Like Pope's lines, the type revealed its creator's ability to fashion a new masterpiece."

28. Hague & Gill (Eric Gill *&* René Hague); Pigotts, England, 1931

AN ESSAY ON TYPOGRAPHY

At first glance, Eric Gill's (1882–1940) *Essay on Typography* appears to be a predictable, workmanlike production, primarily interesting only for its text. Perhaps this impression is due to its size – much like Jan Tschichold's book, *Typographische Gestaltung* (no. 36). The work has typographic ideas aplenty, such as the very modern-looking book jacket that pronounces, "Printing & Piety, an essay of life and works in the England of 1931, and particularly TYPOGRAPHY." On further inspection, however, the book, printed by Gill and his son-in-law, turns out to be a little masterpiece in 120 superb printed pages.

There are twenty-five examples of letterforms in the text, four of which are printed from wood engravings, ranging from Janson to Baskerville to Gill's own Joanna slab-serif type. The text is printed on specially handmade paper of a handsome stone color, bearing Gill's and Hague's initials in the watermark. This was the fourth of their books to be printed on the hand press at Pigotts.

29. Cranach Presse; Weimar, Germany, 1931

CANTICUM CANTICORUM SALOMONIS
Wood engravings by Eric Gill

This beautiful rendering of Solomon's *Song of Songs* was one of the last great works issued by the Cranach Presse. In 1932, Count Kessler was forced to flee the Nazis, bringing a sudden tragic end to the work of the press.

The vertical format of this small book contains eleven sensuous wood engravings by Eric Gill, who also designed the eighteen intricate, decorated initials. The text is printed in Jensen Antiqua type in black, with running heads and titling printed in red, on handmade paper. These engravings are among the most beautiful Gill ever created. There is perfect balance of illustration and text. The small size invites holding and reading, providing an intimate, memorable aesthetic experience. Cranach Presse books are grand but never grandiose; and the *Canticum Canticorum* was a graceful, exquisite coda to the work of a great modern press.

30. Curwen Press; London, England, 1932

SIR THOMAS BROWNE · URNE BURIALL AND THE GARDEN OF CYRUS
Illustrations by Paul Nash

The Curwen Press had a distinguished history before being joined by the Simon brothers, Oliver (1895–1956) and Herbert (1898–1974), in the 1920s. The press had been founded in 1863 by the Reverend John Curwen. Oliver and his brother Herbert were determined to develop the fine printing and aesthetic side of their successful commercial press. Soon after the brothers joined Harold Curwen's establishment they were able to attract the leading artists of the day. As a result, the press became known over the years for its typographic decorations, fine illustrators, decorative papers, and impeccable style.

One example is Thomas Browne's *Urne Buriall*, with its thirty illustrations commissioned from Paul Nash. This project was to receive particular care and attention. John Carter, the distinguished bookman, edited Sir Thomas Browne's text and wrote the introduction. Nash's beautiful drawings were meticulously printed under Herbert's supervision. The illustrations were first printed in collotype, and then watercolor washes were applied to the collotype by pochoir through stencils. It was a painstaking process, and the resulting book was to become much admired and collected.

31. Officina Bodoni (Giovanni Mardersteig); Verona, Italy, 1932

P. OVIDII NASONIS · AMORES

While printing in Switzerland at Montagnola, Giovanni Mardersteig collaborated with the American typographer and designer Frederic Warde. Warde gave Mardersteig the Arrighi type – modeled after the Renaissance italic of Ludovico degli Arrighi – which he had designed, and had had cast in Paris. With this type, and some specially cut calligraphic decoration by the French punchcutter Charles Malin, Mardersteig printed an edition of Ovid's *Amores*.

The Latin text was printed in 120 copies on paper and three on vellum. The beautiful paper was specially made for the Officina by Cartiera Magnani in Brescia. To complement the Arrighi-Vicenza type, Mardersteig designed the title page's calligraphic "Amores," which Malin cut from his lettering. All the copies bear graceful red initial letters handwritten by the calligrapher Claudio Bonacini, both for the part titles and for the fifty-two elegies.

The beauty of the type and the paper, and the perfect printing and spacing of Ovid's verse, combine to create a lyric delicacy of great refinement.

32. Bruce Rogers & Emery Walker; London, England, 1932

T. E. SHAW (trans.) · THE ODYSSEY OF HOMER

After leaving the Riverside Press in 1912, where he had been since 1896, Bruce Rogers began to alternate residence between England and the United States. In 1927, Rogers persuaded T. E. Shaw (Lawrence of Arabia) to translate Homer's *Odyssey.* In the meantime, the Monotype Corporation wanted Rogers to supervise the cutting of his Centaur type, in which the *Odyssey* was to be printed. Therefore, after a brief stay in America, he returned to England in 1928 and proceeded to produce, in addition to the Homer, some of his finest work. Three of his masterpieces from that period are iincluded in this book.

The Odyssey of Homer, the first of this trio, was produced with the financial backing of Colonel Ralph Isham, whose Boswell Papers marked another great printing undertaking with Rogers. Here, B. R. drew roundel designs, derived from Greek vases, which were painstakingly printed in seven separate impressions. The beautifully subtle gray paper was made by the mill of Barcham Green. The resinous, specially prepared, varnish-based ink gave off a delightful aroma, which in some copies is still discernible.

33. The Nonesuch Press (Francis Meynell); London, England, 1933

WILLIAM SHAKESPEARE · THE WORKS OF SHAKESPEARE

Francis Meynell (1891–1975) was born into a distinguished English literary and publishing family. His early career as a printer and designer of books and advertising led by degree to the establishment of his several presses. The Pelican Press was founded first, in 1916, the last, the Nonesuch Press, was established with Vera Mendel and David Garnett, in 1923 and named after Henry VIII's Tudor palace. Their editorial program set them apart from most English private presses whose practice was to reissue classic texts in elaborate garb. It was what Nonesuch published, and the fact that they offered truly new editions, newly edited and often newly discovered, that made the press great.

Meynell chose to make books according to a triple ideal: "significance of subject, beauty of format, and moderation of price." With much hard work, good taste, and careful planning, he succeeded. During a period of fifteen years of publishing, Meynell's press, in Joseph Blumenthal's estimation, "published more than a hundred books which hold their own among the great books of the past." For this accomplishment, Meynell was knighted by the king.

In 1933 the press was to publish (in America, Random House was the press's distributor) a seven-volume *Works of Shakespeare,* printed by Walter Lewis at the University of Cambridge Press. It was, and still remains, a classic, elegant, easy-to-read edition. As Meynell wrote, "Every well-designed book is the begetter of others; and good printing is one of the graces of life even when life is ungracious."

34. Cambridge University Press (Bruce Rogers); Cambridge, England, 1933

STANLEY MORISON · FRA LUCA DE PACIOLI

The second of Bruce Rogers's great books designed during his stay in England in the late 1920s is the magnificent *Fra Luca de Pacioli,* produced for the Grolier Club. The volume, which concerns the construction of roman letters, is based on Pacioli's *De Divina Proportione,* first published in Venice in 1509. This book was to be a companion volume to the Grolier Club's two earlier texts on alphabet construction: Dürer's *Of the Just Shaping of Letters* (1917) and Geofroy Tory's *Champ fleury* (1927).

Rogers used his Monotype Centaur for the text. Following the text, twenty-three letters are printed in a deep, strong black ink on beautiful handmade paper by Batchelor of England. Alphabets by Tagliente and

Palatino are reproduced in four full-page plates. Frederic Goudy designed the small type florets used as ornaments; the line engravings were manufactured by Emery Walker, Ltd. The title page's red and black design, one on which Rogers expended much effort, is surely one of the most magnificent and distinguished of the century. The initial letters were derived from another Pacioli work, the 1494 *Summa de Arithmetica*. Copies in varying colors of florentine figured paper with vellum spine were bound in England by W. H. Smith & Sons.

35. Ashendene Press (C. H. St. John Hornby); Chelsea, England, 1935

A DESCRIPTIVE BIBLIOGRAPHY OF THE BOOKS PRINTED AT THE ASHENDENE PRESS MDCCCXCV–MCMXXXV

Although more than forty years had passed since the printing of Dante's *Divine Comedy* by the Ashendene Press, the quality of their work during that period never varied. The press produced work that was, in the main, allusively Renaissance in inspiration and style. For the most part, the texts chosen by St. John Hornby suited this approach, and his books are steadfastly antiquarian, rather than modern in any real sense. At the time of its closing in 1935, the press issued a beautiful catalogue raisonné of all its work. The book is, in Sir Sydney Cockerell's estimate, "perfect as an example of printing and as a compilation." Indeed, the *Bibliography* sets the tone for later, great bibliographies from other presses, such as that of the Allen Press (no. 84), the Whittington Press (no. 88), and the Grabhorn Press (no. 42).

The specimen pages in the *Bibliography* are mostly accurate resettings of the originals. The collotype process was used for some illustrations, and others were in photogravure, printed by Emery Walker, Ltd. Graily Hewitt provided initials executed by hand. The orderly bibliographic entries required much care, imagination, and skill to make them interesting typographically – perhaps more so than other more determinedly "artistic" productions.

36. Benno Schwabe & Co. (Jan Tschichold); Basel, Switzerland, 1935

JAN TSCHICHOLD · TYPOGRAPHISCHE GESTALTUNG

Jan Tschichold (1902–1974) was born in Leipzig, the eldest son of a sign painter and letter artist. He was one of the first typographers to effectively create designs for the century's first truly "modern-looking" books. As proposed in his book *Die neue Typographie* of 1928, Tschichold attempted to identify what the new typography was. It was to be radically different from previous typography, rejecting all decoration and functioning strictly as an expression of the new machine age. It was to be simple, pure, and universal. Printing was to be asymmetric, because asymmetry was "dynamic," as opposed to "static." Letterforms were to be sans-serif, stripped of nonessential decoration and made of elemental, basic shapes. Tschichold wanted modernist typography to relate and also to reflect to the collateral modernist movement in art.

Tschichold moved to Switzerland in the 1930s, and in 1935 published this small, illustrated work, *Typographische Gestaltung*. In its composition and design, this volume made manifest all that Tschichold had theorized in his attempt to revolutionize book design. The title page is as elegant, fresh, and modern as any he ever did, and the book was widely influential, cited and copied. In the forties, Tschichold came to Britain and redesigned – in his word "reformed" – the design of Allen Lane's famous Penguin books.

37. Oxford University Press (Bruce Rogers); Oxford, England, 1935

THE HOLY BIBLE

The last of the three great books Rogers designed during his mid-1930s stay in England is the majestic lectern *Bible*. The Oxford University Press had traditionally been the publisher of Bibles, noted especially for Bibles print ed for special occasions. Although there are conflicting stories as to the genesis of this Bible, it is generally known to have been the wish of George V to have a lectern Bible made for presentation: a gift for the chapel Canada was to build in Flanders fields as a tribute to the many young soldiers who had died there.

No great pulpit Bible had been printed in England since Baskerville's folio edition of 1763. Humphrey Milford, the press's publisher, along with John Johnston, Printer to the University, invited the much esteemed Rogers – although an American – to design a new lectern Bible using the 1611 King James version as the text.

Rogers immediately set to work, experimenting with one type after another, before finally coming back to his own Centaur, which had to be adapted for his use. The production of the *Bible* was to take five years; a year alone was spent in setting up trial pages. Centaur was employed for all book and chapter headings as well as running heads. Arrighi italic was used for front matter, and Rogers drew new capitals of varying sizes as well. Throughout the years of the *Bible*'s production, Rogers continued to move between America and England. The work was finally issued in one thousand standard folio-size copies on Wolvercote paper and another two hundred larger copies were damp-printed on a handmade Batchelor sheet.

38. The Nonesuch Press (Francis Meynell); London, England, 1936

A. J. A. SYMONS, DESMOND FLOWER, FRANCIS MEYNELL
THE NONESUCH CENTURY

In 1936, the Nonesuch Press issued *The Nonesuch Century*, a celebratory volume of their first one hundred books. An appraisal of the books was written by A. J. A. Symons, with Desmond Flower compiling the bibliography (with, according to the press's director, Francis Meynell, "studiousness and independence of judgment.") Meynell himself wrote notes in the bibliography and discussed the early years of the press in an essay, "The Personal Element." It is a splendid example of the press's output and a handsome bibliography that can hold its own among the great ones of the century. At the time of its publication, the book was lauded in both the London *Times*, by Stanley Morison, and the *New York Times*, by Elmer Adler.

Sadly, even as the *Century* was being published, the the effects of the depression were being felt at the press. Soon after, the press was sold to an American, George Macy, who owned the Limited Editions Club. After World War II, Macy generously returned the use of the "Nonesuch" imprint to Meynell who continued issuing admirable books under this imprint through 1974.

39. Various printers; various places, 1936

DIGGINGS FROM MANY AMPERSANDHOGS

The Typophiles, a distinguished New York-based group of professional and nonprofessional bibliophiles, grew out of a luncheon group that met irregularly during the thirties. Under the informal leadership of Paul A. Bennett, then typographic layout director and later promotion manager of the Mergenthaler Linotype Company, the group ultimately became known as the Typophiles. This informal and ever-changing group has maintained a distinguished history of publications on book-related subjects, starting rather haphazardly in the 1930s as an outgrowth of the printed keepsakes that graced (and still grace) their Christmas luncheons. Thereafter, cooperative printing projects gradually ensued, resulting in the Typophile Chap Books.

In the period from 1935 to 1938, seven books were issued on single themes, an impressive shelf of small and elegantly produced volumes, and, according to Bennett, they "were the most fun." Fun they still are, and a great deal more. Today all of them have become classics, highly sought after and prized for their information as well as their production. The third in the series, *Diggings from many ampersandhogs*, was issued in 1936, the first book concerned entirely with a single typographic subject – in this case, the ampersand. The thirty-five contributed inserts make up a varied and whimsical book of 174 pages. It is a small but delightful *tour de force*.

40. The Gregynog Press; Newton, Wales, 1937

JOHN, LORD OF JOINVILLE · THE HISTORY OF SAINT LOUIS

The Gregynog Press and its related bindery were founded in 1924 by two sisters, Gwendolyn and Margaret Davies, on their estate in rural Wales. It flourished until 1940 when, as with many private enterprises, its production was halted by the advent of World War II. It was, in the words of the printer and printing historian, Joseph Blumenthal, among British private presses – such as Ashendene, Doves, and Eragny – that were "dedicated to grandeur in printing" rather than editorial enterprise.

In the last four years of the press, James Wardrop was in charge. His printing of Joinville's *History,* translated from the French by Joan Evans, was to be among the finest in the press's history. The large colored initials were designed by Alfred J. Fairbanks, and the seventeen armorial shields were engraved in wood by the great woodcut artist Reynolds Stone. The dramatic first text page, printed in three sizes of Poliphilus type, is considered one of the finest openings of twentieth-century British printing.

41. Taylor & Taylor; San Francisco, California, 1939

TYPES BORDERS AND MISCELLANY OF TAYLOR & TAYLOR

The printing firm of Taylor & Taylor had its origins in a prior press established by Edward De Witt Taylor (1871–1962) in 1896, who was later joined by his brother Henry (1879–1937).

By 1939 the firm had printed only about one hundred fine books – a surprisingly small number when compared with other, similar presses. Although prized by California collectors, their printing is not as widely known as it should be, perhaps because their work was done in small editions, and for a mainly San Francisco trade. Taylor & Taylor's *Types Borders and Miscellany* is an exception. More than four hundred alphabets, borders, fleurons, rules, and decorated letters are shown. The work of designers from Amman, Granjon, Tory, and Bell to Koch, Weiss, and Rogers are displayed. The Taylor brothers were deeply interested in the history and evolution of printing, and this superb book is testimony to that involvement.

42. The Grabhorn Press; San Francisco, California, 1940

ELINOR RAAS HELLER AND DAVID MAGEE · BIBLIOGRAPHY OF THE GRABHORN PRESS, 1915–1940

As we have seen in the masterful production of Walt Whitman's *Leaves of Grass* (no. 23), the Grabhorn Press was one of the West Coast's – not to say America's – finest. It was also among the longest-lived of American presses, lasting some forty-five years. Its production was rich and varied, and the Grabhorns printed, in addition to their share of fiction and poetry, a host of fine Americana, much of it Western Californian texts that saw light for the first time under their guidance.

In 1940, the press produced the first of three elegant bibliographies. The first volume, which is displayed here, covers the years up to 1940. An introductory essay was written by Frederic W. Goudy, whose type – the proprietary typeface of the press – was used to print the volume. The beautiful paper is Canson and Montgolfier, made in France. A second bibliography was produced in 1957, with an introduction by Elmer Adler, and a third in 1977, with introductions by Sherwood Grover and Andrew Hoyem, who later merged with and continued the press.

Singly and together, the Grabhorn bibliographies are a typographic monument in the tradition of fine press bibliographies, several of which are included in this exhibition. Clearly, when a fine press decides to print a catalogue of its own work, it puts all possible care and knowledge into the production.

43. Roger Lacourière (plates) and Marthe Fequet & Pierre Baudier (text); Paris, France, 1942

G. L. DE BUFFON · EAUX-FORTES ORIGINALES POUR TEXTES DE BUFFON

Etchings by Pablo Picasso

More than forty years elapsed between the publication of the first *livre d'artiste* in this selection (no. 1), illustrated by Pierre Bonnard, and that of Pablo Picasso's (1881–1973) rendition of G. L. de Buffon's *Histoire Naturelle*. Each of the forty full-page etchings of Buffon's menagerie are rendered with power, freedom, and wit by the artist. The project had been initiated by Vollard, who had been Bonnard's publisher, but he died before the work's completion. Fabriani, an associate of Vollard, took on the project using etchings that Picasso had begun as early as 1936.

Picasso employed a lift ground, or sugar aquatint process, which permitted considerable variety of tone and texture, the better to capture the essence and vitality of each bird and beast. The text and etchings were printed separately, and the work was published, unbound, in portfolio form. The Buffon has often been cited as one of Picasso's finest illustrated books and has also been characterized by Eleanor Garvey as "one of the greatest bestiaries of the 20th century."

44. Bauersche Giesserei; Frankfurt am Main, Germany, 1943

APOKALYPSE

Illustrations by Max Beckmann

The colophon of Max Beckmann's (1884–1950) powerful *Apokalypse* reads: "This book was printed in the first year of the Second World War, as the visions of the apocalyptic seer became dreadful reality." This is all the more forceful a statement when one realizes that it was printed in Germany at the height of the war. Perhaps Beckmann's antiwar sentiments weren't perceived because of the ostensibly religious nature of the *Revelations of Saint John the Evangelist*. Even more astonishing than its publication is that there were available, in the midst of war, the materials, craftsmen, and time needed to produce a work of such demanding complexity.

Beckmann created twenty-seven lithographs, which were printed in black by the Bauersche Giesserei, along with the text in F. H. E. Schneidler's distinctive Legend type. Some of the illustrations were reinterpretations or reworked symbols usually associated with the apocalypse. Out of the small edition of approximately forty, a number were hand colored with watercolor additions executed by Beckmann himself. The copy here illustrated is a special one presented by the artist to his wife.

45. Roger Lacourière (plates) and Georges Girard (text); Paris, France, 1943

FRANÇOIS RABELAIS · PANTAGRUEL

Color woodcuts by André Derain

André Derain (1880–1954) was born in France, and studied art in Paris. For a time he made illustrations for Parisian journals; and then in 1902, began doing book illustration, collaborating with his friend and colleague, Vlaminck. He exhibited his work first with the Fauves and later with the Cubists. Like so many of his French fellow artists, Derain was multitalented, working not only as a painter, but also as sculptor, graphic artist, illustrator, and stage designer as well. The latter three disciplines are evident in his *Pantagruel* of 1943.

For this splendid edition of Rabelais's classic story, Derain created 179 woodcuts, some of which serve as initial letters. The cuts were printed in several colors. An unusual practice in the work is that, instead of using a separate block for each color, a single block was used. This required Derain to cut a white line separating each color area. The blocks were then inked in various colors and printed on dampened paper. It was a laborious process, with the printing taking two years. The result is certainly among the most distinctive and witty *livres d'artiste* of the first half of the century.

46. The Cummington Press (Harry Duncan); Cummington, Massachusetts, 1945

WALLACE STEVENS · ESTHÉTIQUE DU MAL
Drawings by Wightman Williams

Former to his war service and to becoming a printer, Harry Duncan (1916–1997) was an English instructor and poet. During World War II he became increasingly immersed in fine printing, learning a good deal about the craft from the great German émigré artist, Victor Hammer.

The Cummington Press had been founded at the Cummington School of Arts in Massachusetts. In 1945, Duncan produced the *Esthétique du Mal,* a poem by the great American modernist Wallace Stevens. The book is printed in Bruce Rogers's Centaur type and adorned with designs from pen and ink drawings by Wightman Williams. These wonderful, playful renderings of cat's cradles, webbing, and human and animal forms skirt the text, or lie on the bottom or top of the pages, idiosyncratically interchanging with the type, as if each were accommodating the other. They are like "so many sensuous worlds, as if the air, the mid-day air, was swarming with the metaphysical changes that occur."

Although Duncan later moved to Iowa, and then the University of Nebraska, the early books produced in the hill towns of Cummington were simple, dramatic, inventive, and elegant. These works helped set a standard for American printing in the second half of the century.

47. Joh. Enschedé en Zonen (Jan van Krimpen); Haarlem, The Netherlands, 1947

THE BOOK OF PSALMS

Sixteen years after the publication of his design of Homer's *Iliad* and *Odyssey,* Jan van Krimpen designed another book in his Romanée type, a spare and eloquent rendering of *The Book of Psalms.* World War II had recently ended, and factories and basic industries were being rebuilt throughout Europe. It was a time of severe privation combined with a scarcity of materials, makes the printing of such work all the more impressive. The fact that the work has a religious text is also significant.

John Dreyfus shares this opinion and movingly writes in his description of the work: "Of the several postwar examples the most noble is, in my opinion, the edition of *The Book of Psalms.* The type was impeccably printed on English handmade paper and bound in half morocco. In no other setting can the inspiring and consoling quality of the psalms be equally enjoyed after they have once been read in this edition. It is the supreme example of Van Krimpen's success in attaining beauty by skill and modesty in the discharge of his typographical skills." After 1947, Van Krimpen continued to produce fine work until his death in 1958. He has always been justly considered one of this century's great figures of European printing and type design.

48. Edward Vairel (plates) and Draeger Frères (text); Paris, France, 1947

HENRI MATISSE · JAZZ
Illustrations by Henri Matisse

It is unlikely that either Henri Matisse (1869–1954) or his now world-famous book, *Jazz,* will be unfamiliar to the viewer. The book has been reproduced time and again, but as with any great epoch-making work of art, one cannot view the original too often. Matisse's experiments in colored paper cutouts led by degree to their production, in this instance, in pochoir. Pochoir is a stencil technique wherein various colors are applied to a paper surface through a master stencil or screen. It is an extremely painstaking process, requiring repeated applications of different color inks, which usually involved numerous technicians working in stages, each applying a separate color. Matisse, one of the supreme colorists of this century, gloried in the use of brilliant colors, arranged in strong juxtapositions to create dazzling designs. The text, printed in black, recreates the artist's handwriting.

The inspiration for the work is clearly the popular music of the day, and the book translates one medium into another with bravura. There are twenty pochoirs in full color, executed by the artist over a period of two years. If one examines a proof copy, one can see the subtle changes Matisse effected in his desire to achieve the perfect result. The illustrations may look effortless and free, but they are the studied work of a great master.

49. Stamperia del Santuccio (Victor Hammer); Lexington, Kentucky, 1949

J. C. F. HÖLDERLIN · GEDICHTE

Victor Hammer (1882–1967) was born in Austria, where he worked as a painter and art teacher in addition to beginning a career in private press printing and type design. He came to America after being fired from his teaching position by the Nazis. In America he continued to teach art (first at Transylvania College in Kentucky, and later at Wells College in Aurora, New York) and to print fine editions. Many consider this edition of Hölderlin's poems, set in Hammer's third uncial font (named "American Uncial" after his adopted country) and printed on a specially made Magnani paper, his finest production. This folio is the largest format book he ever attempted and displays exceptionally fine hand presswork with unusually deep impression – a trademark of Hammer's books.

50. D. Stempel AG (Hermann Zapf); Frankfurt, Germany, 1949

HERMANN ZAPF & AUGUST ROSENBERGER · FEDER UND STICHEL

Hermann Zapf (born 1918 in Nuremberg, Germany) has combined prodigious skills in the fields of calligraphy, type design, and book design. All of these activities are evident in *Feder und Stichel*, one of Zapf's earliest publications. The twenty-five plates of alphabets and quotations on letters were designed by Zapf from 1939 to 1941 (at the tender age of twenty-three!) and cut by hand in lead with remarkable skill by August Rosenberger, the head punchcutter at the Stempel Type Foundry. This book has been described by no less an authority than the noted German/Swiss typographer Jan Tschichold as one of the most carefully produced volumes on lettering ever published. The seminal Palatino type designed by Zapf is used for the first time in this publication.

51. Mountain House Press (Dard Hunter); Chillicothe, Ohio, 1950

DARD HUNTER · PAPERMAKING BY HAND IN AMERICA

Dard Hunter, Senior (1883–1966) was the twentieth century's leading authority on hand papermaking. He wrote a number books on the subject, most with original specimens or facsimiles of fine paper, and many printed by Hunter himself – some even set in his own hand-cut type font. Some Hunter publications are quite elaborate, but none was more ambitious than this folio edition on the history of hand papermaking in his native country.

This volume has the distinction of being the first – and so far the only – book in the history of printing to be produced entirely by hand and by one person. Hunter not only made the type and paper by hand, but also printed it on a handpress and bound it by hand. The text paper, as well as several of the specimen papers tipped into the volume, were also hand creations of Hunter himself.

52. Anvil Press (Victor Hammer); Lexington, Kentucky, 1953

PICO DELLA MIRANDOLA
ORATIO DE HOMINIS DIGNITATE

The vast majority of Victor Hammer's books were printed in one of the uncial types that he designed: Samson, Pindar, American Uncial, or Andromaque. Occasionally, however, he employed roman or even black letter types. The Anvil Press edition of *Oration on the Dignity of Man* is set by hand in two roman fonts: Joseph Blumenthal's Spiral type is used for the Latin text, with ATF Garamond for the English. The capitals on the title page have been reworked with a graver by Hammer to achieve a sharper and somewhat more calligraphic effect. As with most Hammer productions, the paper is a beautiful handmade sheet, and the presswork is uniform and characteristically deep.

53. D. Stempel AG (Hermann Zapf); Frankfurt, Germany, 1954

HERMANN ZAPF · MANUALE TYPOGRAPHICUM

From 1939 to 1960 Hermann Zapf designed many typefaces for the Stempel Typefoundry of Frankfurt, Germany, including some of the most popular and successful of the century, including such familiar names as Palatino (released in 1948), Melior (1950), and Optima (1958). Zapf was also art director of the house printing office at Stempel from 1947 to 1956. In 1954, after years of work, Zapf's first *Manuale Typographicum* was published. Expanding on the concept of previous type specimen books, Zapf here employed his own, as well as other, types manufactured by the Stempel foundry in a series of one hundred purely typographic arrangements. It is a display of typographic inventiveness and variety that has never been surpassed. The skill and dexterity of the typesetting and presswork are extraordinary.

54. The Plantin Press (Saul & Lillian Marks); Los Angeles, California, 1955

JAMES R. PAGE · A DESCRIPTIVE CATALOGUE OF THE BOOK
OF COMMON PRAYER

Saul Marks, an immigrant from Poland, founded the Plantin Press with his wife, Lillian, in Detroit in 1928, moving it to California in 1930. In Los Angeles the Plantin Press developed a reputation for careful typesetting, innovative use of ornament, and exemplary presswork – all of which are evident in this volume. Like the Merrymount and Spiral presses, Plantin was able to achieve these results – results that rival the work of the great private presses – in a commercial setting.

This book is set mainly in Bembo, with characteristically tight word spacing – a hallmark of the Plantin Press. Marks has skillfully combined it with an assortment of other fonts to achieve a seemingly effortless type page. The average text page incorporates Alfred Fairbank's Narrow Bembo Italic, Eric Gill's Perpetua Titling initials, and Bell brackets, in addition to Bembo roman and italic – to say nothing of Poliphilus hyphens and an attractive pair of ornaments.

55. The St. Albert's Press (William Everson); San Francisco, California, 1955

NOVUM PSALTERIUM PII XII

William Everson (1912–1994) certainly had one of the more unusual and varied careers of any printer. Perhaps best known as a poet, Everson was also a monk (Brother Antoninus) for a good part of his life, including the period when he worked on the printing of this Psalter. Hand setting the book in 18-point Goudy Newstyle type and printing the folio pages on a handpress using dampened handmade Barcham Green paper proved to be a monumental undertaking for Everson. Indeed, the task was too daunting, and only a portion of the work was ever completed and issued in 1955 with the support of Estelle Doheny. But even as a fragment, it is a noble book, and one of the major achievements in fine printing of the century.

56. Officina Bodoni (Giovanni Mardersteig); Verona, Italy, 1956

LUCA PACIOLI · DE DIVINA PROPORTIONE

Among other careers, Fra Luca da Pacioli was a monk and mathematician. His alphabet of constructed roman capitals was reproduced by the Grolier Club, with an introduction by Stanley Morison and typography by Bruce Rogers, in their justly famous edition of 1933 (no. 34 in this catalogue). Mardersteig's edition of Pacioli's work concerns his texts on geometric constructions other than the alphabet. In this volume the text is perfectly hand printed in Bembo type and contains a section of color reproductions of three-dimensional renderings of the geometric constructions (which may have been made originally by Leonardo da Vinci). The occasional fine-line diagrams in the margins of the type pages make for an unusually handsome text page.

57. Adrian Wilson; San Francisco, California, 1957

ADRIAN WILSON · PRINTING FOR THEATER

Adrian Wilson (1923–1988) spent most of his career as a freelance designer and printer. He was married to an actress, Joyce Lancaster, and for some years he printed charming announcements for the semiprofessional theater of which she was a member. Many of these announcements were put together with great haste since the bill was often not known until just before the performance. They were printed on odd lots of paper the Wilsons were able to acquire on a small budget. Despite this – or perhaps because of it – there is a zest and exuberance to these ephemeral pieces that put them in a class by themselves. In 1957 Wilson combined a large number of the announcements in a noble folio volume, set in Caslon and Trajanus types and printed on hand-made Tovil paper – a sumptuous setting for their playful and inspired ephemera.

58. Overbrook Press (Thomas Maitland Cleland); Stamford, Connecticut, 1958

L'ABBÉ PRÉVOST · HISTOIRE DU CHEVALIER DES GRIEUX ET DE MANON LESCAUT
Serigraphs by T. M. Cleland

Thomas Maitland Cleland was one of the notable designers of what may be called America's golden age of typography: the period from about the turn of the century to the middle 1900s. This period includes such luminaries as D. B. Updike (born 1860), Frederic W. Goudy (born 1865), Will Bradley (born 1868), Bruce Rogers (born 1870), W. A. Dwiggins (born 1880), and Rudolf Ruzicka (born 1883). A wide variety of Cleland's work is shown in the Pynson Printers' compendium, published in 1929 (no. 19).

Cleland's work was allusive in nature, harking back to a variety of styles, including the Renaissance and Baroque; but he was most satisfied when working in a colorful French rococo manner. For this edition of *Manon Lescaut,* Overbrook Press proprietor Frank Altschul offered Cleland the opportunity to design and illustrate a book exactly as he wished, sparing no amount of effort, time, or expense. Cleland combined silk-screen illustrations with the letterpress text printed in Caslon type. The edition, containing 230-odd drawings, and using a minimum of six colors each, and therefore at least six screens, is a masterpiece of refined bookmaking.

59. Stamperia Valdonega (Giovanni Mardersteig); Verona, Italy, 1958

OVID · METAMORPHOSES
Etchings by Hans Erni

The Limited Editions Club was founded in New York by George Macy in 1929, just before the stock market crash. The club managed to persevere in its original form into the 1970s, producing well-made editions of the world's classics, not a few of which can be considered among the finest and most affordable volumes of fine printing of their time. Many of the twentieth century's finest typographers and illustrators produced books for the LEC, including Bruce Rogers, D. B. Updike, Joseph Blumenthal, Francis Meynell, Will Carter, Jan van Krimpen, E. R. Weiss, and Giovanni Mardersteig, who designed eighteen books for the club. The earliest of these were overseen by Mardersteig at the Officina Bodoni but printed elsewhere (despite the somewhat misleading imprint and colophon information). After 1948 the LEC volumes were printed under Mardersteig's direct supervision at his own machine press operation in Verona, the Stamperia Valdonega.

This edition of Ovid's *Metamorphoses,* set in Centaur type, contains fifteen line etchings by the noted Swiss artist Hans Erni. The artwork, typography, and binding combine to make a beautiful and harmonious whole.

60. The Hammer Creek Press (John Fass); New York, New York, 1958

THE ALPHABET IN VARIOUS ARRANGEMENTS

John Fass worked in commercial printing and typography from the 1920s until his death in 1966, but admirers of fine printing are most enthusiastic about the small hand-produced books from his Hammer Creek Press issued in tiny editions beginning in the early 1950s. On a small handpress (which at one time was owned by Bruce Rogers), Fass printed about thirty thoroughly charming books and many pieces of ephemera. Most, like *The Alphabet in Various Arrangements*, were produced in exceedingly limited editions and given away to friends. This edition is one of the smallest, with only eight copies made, though a few Hammer Creek items were issued in an edition of one! A surprisingly small number of types are used to print this colorful variety of typographic arrangements of the alphabet. The limited type repertoire was a necessity for Fass – he lived and printed in one room at the YMCA, storing the type cases under his bed.

61. Trajanus Presse (Gotthard de Beauclair); Frankfurt, Germany, 1960

DAS EVANGELIUM JOHANNES

Gotthard de Beauclair was among the more influential European book designers of the twentieth century. As head designer at the German publishing house founded by Anton Kippenberg, Insel Verlag, he designed (mostly anonymously) hundreds of books admired around the world for their clarity and beauty. Included among them are the handsome series of small, uniform-format editions, the "Insel Bücherei." But de Beauclair's book design activities were not limited to the Insel house alone; he also designed books for several other publishers, including a few fine press imprints. The first of these private imprints was the Trajanus Press, set up by the Stempel Type Foundry in Frankfurt to give de Beauclair the opportunity of printing exceptional books in the fine press tradition. Sixteen titles were published, all displaying exceptionally careful typography and superior presswork. *Das Evangelium Johannes,* set in Hermann Zapf's Aldus and Heraklit Greek types, is among the most impressive of them. Notable in this volume are the specially made Hahnemuhle paper and the beautiful full-leather binding by Willy Pingel of Heidelberg.

62. Officina Bodoni (Giovanni Mardersteig); Verona, Italy, 1960

FELICE FELICIANO (G. Mardersteig, ed.) · ALPHABETUM ROMANUM

Giovanni Mardersteig's Officina Bodoni was one of the longest-lived (1923–1977) and surely one of the most respected handpresses of the century. Mardersteig was born in Germany where he began his career in printing and publishing. For health reasons he later moved to Switzerland, and then in 1927 on to Verona, where he was to spend the rest of his life. Several important books were produced by Mardersteig before the war, many in authentic Bodoni types cast from the original matrices – hence the name "Officina Bodoni." After the war, and with the founding of a machine press operation, the Stamperia Valdonega, situated just down the hill from his hand press, Mardersteig's printing activities came to full fruition.

Several of his publications concerned the Renaissance antiquary, alchemist, and eccentric, Felice Feliciano (born 1433), whose alphabet of constructed roman capitals (one of the earliest of its kind, dating from circa 1460) is reproduced in *Alphabetum Romanum*. The book is set in Mardersteig's own Dante font and contains re-drawings of Feliciano's capitals, each hand colored in hues to match the delightful variety of the original manuscript that is one of the treasures of the Vatican Library.

63. Bauersche Giesserei; Frankfurt am Main, Germany, 1961

AM WEGESRAND
Woodcuts by Fritz Kredel

The calligrapher George Salter and the illustrator Fritz Kredel were leaders in their respective fields. Both were expatriate Germans, forced to emigrate by the Nazis, who made America their adopted homeland. They remained close friends in New York City, where both had settled, and where both worked mainly for New York-based publishers. Salter created hundreds of dust jackets and designed many publications, and Kredel's illustrations graced more than four hundred volumes. A comprehensive exhibition of Kredel's work was held at the Grolier Club in 2001. *Am Wegesrand* was a labor of love for the two friends, containing hand-colored woodcuts of local plants by Kredel, with the text from related poems flowing around the images in Salter's elegant calligraphy. The pair were fortunate in having their work printed by the Bauer Typefoundry on a fine mould-made paper, with a handsome binding in quarter-vellum and silk sides by Willy Pingel.

64. Ludwig Oehms (Hermann Zapf); Frankfurt, Germany, 1962

KARL GRUBER · ASCHAFFENBURG

The authors take pleasure in noting that, in addition to numerous monumental folios, there are several diminutive volumes included in this selection that display some of the finest bookmaking of the twentieth century. This little volume on the German town of Aschaffenburg for Hermann Emig in the Oldenwald is one example. The proportions, paper (a pleasant machine-made sheet), and production (Linotype composition for the letterpress text, and offset for the illustrations) are unpretentious. The elegance of design and extraordinary care in the details of bookmaking make this an exceptional volume, set in Zapf's Aldus and well printed by Ludwig Oehms in Frankfurt. The carefully selected illustrations are tipped in throughout the book. The binding is the one element that could possibly be called sumptuous, executed in half-vellum with refined small corner tips, and a lovely orange/red paste paper decorated in gold – all by Willy Pingel of Heidelberg.

Aschaffenburg is one of the first volumes in a series of nearly forty books designed by Zapf for Emig. It is a prime example of how proportion, beautiful design, and care in the small, often unnoticed details of bookmaking can make a masterpiece of a small volume.

65. The Spiral Press (Joseph Blumenthal); New York, New York, 1962

LAURENCE SICKMAN (ed.) · CHINESE CALLIGRAPHY AND PAINTING IN THE COLLECTION OF JOHN M. CRAWFORD, JR.

Joseph Blumenthal founded the Spiral Press in 1926 with a partner, Georg Hoffmann, who left the firm during the Great Depression. Over the course of more than four decades the press produced some of the finest books in the United States, respected the world over for the taste and high standards of craftsmanship they exemplified. From the beginning, Blumenthal espoused a modern typographic style, going against the tide of allusive and anachronistic typography embraced by others of his generation.

In *Chinese Calligraphy and Painting,* Blumenthal employed the Sistina type, designed by Hermann Zapf, in combination with Intertype Garamond. The multicolor illustrations were printed by Arthur Jaffé, and the monochrome plates were printed in collotype by the Meriden Gravure Company on the same Caledonia Parchment paper onto which the Spiral Press impressed the letterpress text with customary skill. Blumenthal has said that if he "were asked by a harassed St. Peter outside the Pearly Gates to show only one printed book on which [he] should be judged," this would be it.

66. D. Stempel AG (Hermann Zapf); Frankfurt, Germany, 1963

HERMANN ZAPF · TYPOGRAPHIC VARIATIONS

This compilation of seventy-eight book and title pages designed by Hermann Zapf was printed by the Stempel Type Foundry in 1963. It was the last great collaboration between the brilliant typographer and the proprietary printing office which he had helped develop for the Stempel foundry.

Most of the pages in this volume are resettings in Stempel types of various books that Zapf had designed since 1949; others were designed specially for this edition. As with other Zapf/Stempel productions, the typesetting and presswork are superlative, to say nothing of the inventiveness of the myriad designs. The edition was bound by Willy Pingel in quarter vellum.

67. The Stone Wall Press (Kim Merker); Iowa City, Iowa, 1963

THEODORE ROETHKE · SEQUENCE, SOMETIMES METAPHYSICAL
Wood engravings by John Roy

Kim K. Merker, a student of Harry Duncan (see nos. 46 and 97), preserves elements of Duncan's style – such as the use of classical types (particularly those of Jan van Krimpen), quality paper, and clear, unornamented typography. But he quickly developed his own distinctive style, and this early production – the seventh from Merker's Stone Wall Press – shows all the elements of his mature style: elegant typography in Jan van Krimpen's Romanée and Open Kapitalen fonts, innovative handling of woodcut illustrations printed on a lightweight Japanese paper, and meticulous, lightly-inked presswork on imported Rives paper – all in a simple yet elegant binding of Fabriano paper-covered boards, stamped in gold on the spine.

68. The Spiral Press (Joseph Blumenthal); New York, New York, 1965

ECCLESIASTES
Drawings by Ben Shahn

Joseph Blumenthal collaborated on significant books with many important artists at his Spiral Press. Among them were Max Weber, Alexander Calder, Antonio Frasconi, and Ben Shahn, with whom he worked on *The Alphabet of Creation* and this deluxe edition of *Ecclesiastes.* Both titles were hand set in Blumenthal's own Emerson type. For the *Ecclesiastes* edition, Shahn's drawings were skillfully cut in wood by Stefan Martin and printed on Rives paper. The quarter-vellum binding, with its solander and slipcases covered in Fabriano paper, was executed by Blumenthal's favorite binder, the Russell-Rutter Company.

69. The Rampant Lions Press (Will Carter); Cambridge, England, 1965

ARMIDA MARIA-THERESA COLT · WEEDS AND WILDFLOWERS
Wood engravings by George Mackley

Will Carter and his talented son, Sebastian, have produced some of the finest typographic designs and press-work of postwar England – all from a surprisingly small workshop in their home. When their skills as printers were combined with the exceptional talents of wood engraver George Mackley, the results were extraordinary. Carter's meticulous printing brings out all the detail and beauty of Mackley's accomplished engravings. The delicate and refined Arrighi typeface is the perfect complement to Mackley's sensitive and detailed work.

70. Gehenna Press (Leonard Baskin); Northampton, Massachusetts, 1967

FLOSCULI SENTENTIARUM

Leonard Baskin began printing while he was an art student at Yale University in the 1940s. In 1942 he founded the Gehenna Press, under which imprint emanated fine editions for the rest of the century. Most of the books were illustrated with original graphics – mostly by Baskin himself (see, for example, no. 96) – but occasionally he produced a purely typographic book such as this one. This collection contains arrangements of types and ornaments that once belonged to Bruce Rogers and now resides, as does the Grabhorn archive, at Yale University's Sterling Library. The sumptuous paper was hand made in France in 1905. Baskin himself refers to the book as a *"tour de force,"* also saying that he had "ever been interested in these marvelous flowers that grow in the hidden garden of printers' cases, & their use, both scant & profuse, by early printers."

71. Trajanus Presse (Gotthard de Beauclair); Frankfurt, Germany, 1966

JOSEPH BÉDIER (Rudolf G. Bindings, trans.) · DER ROMAN VON TRISTAN UND ISOLDE
Woodcuts by Fritz Kredel

The book designer Gotthard de Beauclair (1902–1992) and the illustrator Fritz Kredel (1900–1973) are two of the towering figures of twentieth-century book design. Both men were at one time members of Rudolf Koch's Offenbach Werkstatt, though Kredel was certainly the more active. Kredel, who had married a Jewish woman employed in the workshop to weave tapestries for Koch, fled the Nazis and settled in New York, collaborating with de Beauclair and Kredel on a few projects after the war. Among them were a book on dolls and puppets for Joseph Graves's Gravesend Press and some Insel Verlag publications; but this volume, printed on mould-made paper, with Kredel's woodcuts colored by hand, is the most elaborate. A third German-born book artist, Jan Tschichold, designed the important Sabon typeface that is used here for the first time. When this book was printed in 1966, only the 10-point roman font was ready, so de Beauclair ingeniously used color and the Alte Schwabacher as a display type for headings. The printer Walter Wilkes hand set most of the type for this edition early in his career.

72. The Plantin Press (Saul & Lillian Marks); Los Angeles, California, 1967

RICHARD E. LINGENFELTER · PRESSES OF THE PACIFIC ISLANDS 1817–1867

This smaller volume displays the same care in typography and presswork as the Plantin Press's large quarto volume, the *Descriptive Catalogue of the Book of Common Prayer* (No. 54). As in that larger volume, the materials used here are exceptional (Rives paper, natural linen cloth binding, etc.), but in this case the book has been published by the Plantin Press itself. The woodcuts by Edgar Dorset Taylor are tastefully printed on Japanese paper and the offset illustrations, scattered throughout the book, add variety to an attractive and useful volume.

73. Oxford University Press (Stanley Morison); Oxford, England, 1967
STANLEY MORISON · JOHN FELL

Stanley Morison relished large folio volumes on the history of printing. From *Four Centuries of Fine Printing* (1926) through folio histories on German incunabula, to the printing of *The History of the Times,* Morison lavished great care and expense on such books. This volume on John Fell, the Oxford bishop who imported an assortment of Continental types for use at the Oxford University Press, is exceptional for a postwar book, for every one of its 278 folio pages was set entirely by hand and carefully printed on a beautiful English handmade paper – all done, appropriately enough, at the Oxford University Press. *John Fell* was the last – and some would say the finest – of the noble folios by this great printing historian. He was born on May 6, 1889 (the feast of Saint John *ante portam latinum,* the patron saint of printers and scribes), and died on October 11, 1967, the day before the book's official publication date.

74. The Adagio Press (Leonard Bahr); Harper Woods, Michigan, 1969
NORMAN H. STROUSE AND JOHN DREYFUS · C-S THE MASTER CRAFTSMAN

It is difficult for a small, after-hours press to compete with the finest printers of this century, but a select few, such as John Fass's Hammer Creek Press and Leonard Bahr's Adagio Press, reached such heights. This slim folio, handset in Palatino and Pascal types and hand printed one page at a time on a platen press on Tovil handmade paper, is a major achievement. Every aspect of this book is of the highest caliber – from the important texts by John Dreyfus and Norman Strouse to the original Doves Press leaves and quarter-vellum binding with marbled-paper sides executed by Fritz and Trudi Eberhardt. Bahr is noted for his fresh, modern typography and his lavish use of color. Almost every page of this hand-printed volume is in three colors with an unusually large head margin occupied by the colorful running heads.

75. David R. Godine (David Godine & Lance Hidy); Boston, Massachusetts, 1970
ANDREW MARVELL · THE GARDEN
Etchings by Lance Hidy

Another charming yet small volume is this early publication from David R. Godine (publisher of the book you are now reading). The early works from Godine's press were the result of very young and totally inexperienced printers working in an atmosphere of communal disorder. Lance Hidy (the illustrator of this volume), Michael Bixler, Susan Warde, Martha Rockwell, and Katy Homans were among the principal participants in the production of some exceptional publications. In this volume, Jan van Krimpen's elegant Cancelleresca Bastarda type harmonizes beautifully with Lance Hidy's delicate etchings, all printed on a soft, handmade Italian paper and bound in linen over boards.

76. Cherryburn Press (R. Hunter Middleton); Chicago, Illinois, 1970
JAMES M. WELLS · A PORTFOLIO OF THOMAS BEWICK WOOD ENGRAVINGS

It was quite a coup when R. Hunter Middleton acquired over 150 original Thomas Bewick woodblocks in the 1940s. Over the years Middleton (who was director of type design for the Ludlow Corporation in Chicago) printed assorted books with the blocks, expending more care on the makeready and presswork than had ever been lavished in Bewick's own time. This portfolio contains the most complete collection of the blocks in Middleton's possession, painstakingly printed on Hosho paper, and contained in a box made by the fine bookbinder, Elizabeth Kner.

77. The Trianon Press (Arnold Fawcus); Paris, France, 1972

GEOFFREY KEYNES · WILLIAM BLAKE'S WATER-COLOUR DESIGNS FOR THE POEMS OF THOMAS GRAY

Beginning in 1957, to mark the bicentenary of William Blake's birth, Arnold Fawcus's Paris-based Trianon Press published a series of facsimiles of Blake's works. The volumes issued achieve new heights of fidelity and standards of production. Most have been printed on specially made Arches paper and bound in quarter-leather with hand-marbled paper sides. The first title in the series was Blake's *Illustrations to the Bible,* reproducing nearly two hundred paintings. The Trianon edition of *Songs of Innocence and Experience* contains fifty-four plates, averaging a remarkable thirty-four colors per plate, but that prodigious amount of work almost pales in comparison to the 116 images reproduced in twenty-five to forty-two colors applied by pochoir for this volume, making these three folio volumes the grandest of this grand series. The fidelity of the reproductions was so high that no one referring to the originals and the facsimiles, placed side by side, could tell the difference.

78. Officina Bodoni (Giovanni Mardersteig); Verona, Italy, 1973

THE FABLES OF AESOP

This edition of Aesop's *Fables* was one of the last great books printed by Giovanni Mardersteig on the hand-presses of his Officina Bodoni. Throughout the history of the press Mardersteig would often reproduce illustrations made for early editions of a book, but he would never allow himself to simply use photo-mechanical means of reproduction. Instead, for books such as *The Nymphs of Fiesole, The Four Gospels,* and this edition of *Aesop's Fables*, with sixty-eight woodcuts from a fifteenth-century edition, Mardersteig had the illustrations recut on wood by hand by Anna Bramanti.

Mardersteig found a unique contemporary hand-colored copy of the original edition at the British Museum, which is the basis for the hand coloring of this edition by Daniel Jacomet of Paris. The ornaments used throughout the book are based on those first made by the printer of the Veronese Aesop, Giovanni Alvise, and the translation by William Caxton is from the first English edition.

79. Plain Wrapper Press (Richard-Gabriel Rummonds & Alessandro Zanella); Verona, Italy, 1974

JORGE LUIS BORGES · SIETE POEMAS SAJONES/SEVEN SAXON POEMS
Relief images by Arnaldo Pomodoro

In the 1996 publication on the work of the Plain Wrapper Press, *A Sampler of Leaves*, Decherd Turner assessed the Plain Wrapper Press edition of *Seven Saxon Poems* and concluded that it compared favorably with an illustrious predecessor, the Kelmscott Chaucer. While some may consider his assessment a bit too enthusiastic, it nevertheless indicates how impressive a book the Borges is. The paper, presswork, title-page calligraphy, and inventive use of Arnaldo Pomodoro's designs (in particular on the binding, where they are reproduced in gold-plated bronze relief) all make for a particularly luxurious volume. Through thirty-eight publications, Richard-Gabriel Rummonds and his partner, Alessandro Zanella, maintained a high level of book production on their handpresses, at a time when conditions were hardly favorable for such elaborate productions. It created something of a stir when the title was issued with a four-digit publication price.

Unfortunately, the trying nature of private press printing caused Rummonds and Zanella to dissolve the Plain Wrapper Press in 1988, with Rummonds going on to teach and publish books under the Ex-Ophidia imprint (now also defunct) in Alabama, and Zanella continuing to print in Verona, Italy.

80. The Rampant Lions Press (Will & Sebastian Carter); Cambridge, England, 1974

WILLIAM MORRIS · THE STORY OF CUPID AND PSYCHE
Illustrations by William Morris & Edward Burne-Jones

This 1974 publication of William Morris's translation of *The Story of Cupid and Psyche* was more than a hundred years in the making. It began in the 1860s when Edward Burne-Jones drew forty-four illustrations for the story. William Morris, then working with the Chiswick Press, was dissatisfied with the types available, so he abandoned the project. The weak modern-style types available in the mid-ineteenth century were too light in combination with the strong wood engravings. It was only when Morris founded his private press and had his own proprietary typefacecs cut that a suitable combination was possible. In 1969, after hearing a talk by Colin Franklin, Will and Sebastian Carter became intrigued by the aborted project. They received permission from the Society of Antiquaries and the Ashmolean Museum to print from the original woodblocks. Since the Carters found that most types did not work well with the heavy engravings, they also sought – and got – permission from Cambridge University to recast type from Morris's original Troy type matrices for setting the poem.

The end result is a beautiful book, following Morris's style just enough to look "right," while also combining all the elements in a novel way, making this a quintessential Rampant Lions Press book. Here, as in *Weeds and Wildflowers* (no. 69), one can see the results of the Carters' impeccable presswork – all the more remarkable considering that this book was printed two pages up on a platen press.

81. Cantz'sche Druckerei (Jan Tschichold; Berzona, Switzerland); Stuttgart, Germany, 1975

JAN TSCHICHOLD (ed.) · DAS SCHREIBBUCH DES VESPASIANO AMPHIAREO

The Amphiareo volume is a prime example of Jan Tschichold's elegant later typography, a style representing a highly evolved classicism. The perfect letter spacing of the all-cap lines and careful handling of all typographic elements, down to the smallest details of punctuation and optical alignment, are Tschichold hallmarks. As with all of Tschichold's work, the small, often unnoticed details of book production (such as proper paper grain and even, precise presswork) are carefully thought through and attended to. This book also benefits from a fine Fabriano text paper and handsome half-vellum binding with small, delicate vellum corner tips and Douglas Cockerell marbled paper sides.

82. Joh. Enschedé en Zonen (Bram de Does); Haarlem, The Netherlands, 1978

CHARLES ENSCHEDÉ (Harry Carter, trans.) · TYPEFOUNDRIES IN THE NETHERLANDS

Since the 1920s there had been plans to publish an English edition of Charles Enschedé's monumental work on type founding in the Netherlands. For this book, which was finally published in 1978, Bram de Does designed an extraordinary edition, hand set in Jan van Krimpen's Romanée type and printed letterpress on a beautiful mold-made paper. The volume contains 519 examples printed from original material at the Enschedé foundry, including specimens of some unique types – dating back hundreds of years – that were specially recast for this edition. As with Morison's *John Fell* (no. 73, printed by the Oxford University Press), the scale and effort of handsetting hundreds of folio pages and printing them by letterpress – particularly at such a late date – represents an extraordinary, and probably not to be repeated, accomplishment. The foundry closed its doors recently and the types and matrices were dispersed or destroyed.

83. Arion Press (Andrew Hoyem); San Francisco, California, 1979

HERMAN MELVILLE · MOBY-DICK; OR, THE WHALE
Wood engravings by Barry Moser

This 1979 edition of Melville's classic was a seminal publication for both Andrew Hoyem's Arion Press and the talented wood engraver, Barry Moser. The folio volume, handset in Goudy Modern type, printed damp on handmade paper and with one hundred wood engravings by Moser, was a huge undertaking for a private press in the 1970s. The result has been acclaimed as one of the finest – if not the finest – efforts from the West Coast's Arion Press and the East Coast's Barry Moser. The favorable publicity and reviews the book received helped propel the careers of both to new heights (see also nos. 86 & 92 below).

84. The Allen Press (Lewis & Dorothy Allen); Greenbrae, California, 1981

THE ALLEN PRESS BIBLIOGRAPHY

Beginning in 1939 Lewis and Dorothy Allen began issuing luxurious limited-edition books printed by hand. Their materials were deluxe, their types classic, and their craftsmanship impeccable. This 1981 bibliography displayed the Allen Press and their talents at their best, utilizing materials seen in their finest publications: handmade Barcham Green paper, handset typ,; and specially blocked Fortuny binding fabric. The layout and typography also represent the best of the press (particularly the delightful hand-colored title-page reusing a Mallette Dean woodblock from their 1960 publication, *The Splendid Idle Forties*). This bibliography was the last book printed on the Allens' large Columbian press; subsequent Allen Press books were printed on a smaller Albion Press. The type, Van Krimpen's Romanée, is a design that was not particularly successful commercially but was used for a surprising number of volumes in this catalogue (see nos. 27, 47, 67, and 82).

85. The Windhover Press (Kim Merker); Iowa City, Iowa, 1981

ANONYMOUS (W. S. Merwin, trans.) · ROBERT THE DEVIL
Woodcuts by Roxanne Sexauer

For this edition of W. S. Merwin's translation of a medieval play, Merker enlisted the assistance of Roxanne Sexauer, who has created woodcuts in a medieval "spirit." The type is Mardersteig's Dante, with Bembo italic and Centaur capitals for display; the paper was specially hand made for the press in England. As with all of Merker's books, there is a combination of beautiful and legible classicism with an inventive and fresh approach. The type and general handling of the text are traditional, but the asymmetric title page using a woodcut line border is novel. A special deluxe issue of fifty copies, with the woodcuts hand colored by the artist, is one of the more attractive – and rare – of the Windhover publications.

86. Arion Press (Andrew Hoyem); San Francisco, California, 1982

APOCALYPSE: THE REVELATION OF SAINT JOHN
THE DIVINE
Woodcuts by Jim Dine

Following the success of its edition of *Moby-Dick,* Andrew Hoyem's Arion Press went on to publish numerous books in the *livres d'artiste* tradition with illustrations by such noted artists as Willem de Kooning, Robert

Motherwell, and Jim Dine. The latter created expressionist woodcuts to illustrate this edition of the *Apocalypse*. The book is printed on a sumptuous, rough Richard de Bas paper – a stock perfectly suited to the strong, vigorous and roughly hewn artwork, but still a challenging printing surface. The uncovered wood boards and pigskin spine make a fitting package for the contents.

87. The Perishable Press Limited (Walter Hamady); Mount Horeb, Wisconsin, 1982

WALTER HAMADY · PAPERMAKING BY HAND

Many in the fine printing community rate Walter Hamady's presswork superlative. Another of Hamady's skills was papermaking. This publication combines these two extraordinary talents in a wonderful way. The type was entirely hand set in Hermann Zapf's Palatino font, with Hamady rewriting his text as needed to eliminate broken words throughout the book. Printed on an assortment of handmade stocks, including several made by Hamady himself, the book contains the added bonus of a beautiful calligraphic title page by Hermann Zapf, that plays well against the handsome typographic title page by Hamady. The careful reader will notice that the two pages have different titles: the typographic version has "Hand Papermaking" as the title, while Zapf's calligraphy spells out "Papermaking by Hand."

88. The Whittington Press (John & Rosalind Randle); Andoversford, England, 1982

DAVID BUTCHER AND JOHN RANDLE · THE WHITTINGTON PRESS: A BIBLIOGRAPHY, 1971–1981

Since 1971, John and Rosalind Randle have been producing editions in the finest private-press tradition at their Whittington Press in the Cotswolds. High-quality papers (handmade, mould made, and machine made) combined with fine Monotype faces – including their perennial favorite, Caslon – are Whittington trademarks. Their folio bibliography is ample testimony to a publishing program of the highest caliber, and including many important contributions to the literature of fine printing. In addition to their books, they publish the commendable and handsome journal *Matrix*, an indispensable compilation of printing articles, essays, and specimens issued annually since 1981.

89. Iowa Center for the Book (Kim Merker); Iowa City, Iowa, 1983

SAMUEL BECKETT · COMPANY

It is a tribute to Kim Merker's efforts and organizational ability that his three books in this volume – *Sequence, Sometimes Metaphysical; Robert the Devil;* and *Company* – have been issued under three different imprints: The Stone Wall Press, The Windhover Press, and the Iowa Center for the Book, respectively. *Company* was the first book published by the Iowa Center for the Book, and it is clear that they wanted to initiate their publication program with a splash. The volume is sumptuous in every way, from its scale (small folio) and Arches paper, to the prints of intaglio etchings by Dallas Henke, and half-leather binding by the late Bill Anthony. The type, Jan van Krimpen's Spectrum, looks particularly handsome in the large 18-point size, beautifully printed here on the Arches paper.

90. Meriden-Stinehour Press (Eleanor Caponigro); Meriden, Connecticut, & Lunenburg, Vermont, 1983

SARAH GREENOUGH AND JUAN HAMILTON
ALFRED STIEGLITZ: PHOTOGRAPHS & WRITINGS

Meriden-Stinehour Press, formerly two separate companies that merged in 1975 to operate under the name of the Stinehour Press, has specialized in fine art reproduction in general – and the reproduction of photographs in particular – since the earlier part of the century. Many innovations in fine printing have been pioneered by the firm, including the use of extra-fine line screens, and tritone reproductions of black and white photographs for extra richness and tonal range. This book is one of the first uses of tritone offset printing, where a black and two other colors (usually two grays, but sometimes a brown, blue, yellow, etc.) are combined to reproduce an image. The paper was specially made in a heavy weight and rough finish by the Mohawk papermill – a challenge to the printer that was aptly met throughout the book to approximate the tonal range of Stieglitz's work. Eleanor Caponigro's elegant design, using Monotype Bembo for the letterpress text, results in an exceptionally beautiful book. All in all, this volume is a fitting tribute to Stieglitz's genius.

91. Stamperia Valdonega (Martino Mardersteig); Verona, Italy, 1983
PIETRO NANIN · LO SPLENDORE DELLA VERONA AFFRESCATA

Martino Mardersteig has carried on in the great letterpress tradition of his father, Giovanni Mardersteig (1891–1977), founder of the Officina Bodoni and Stamperia Valdonega. To that legacy Martino has added the extra dimension of offset printing. This folio volume exhibits the finest of the Stamperia Valdonega's letterpress *and* multicolor offset work. The type is Monotype Dante, designed by Giovanni Mardersteig; the illustrations were reproduced one color at a time on Heidelberg offset presses. The presswork – both letterpress and offset – is of the highest quality, and the design clear and classic.

92. Pennyroyal Press (Barry Moser); Northampton, Massachusetts, 1983
MARY SHELLEY · FRANKENSTEIN; OR, THE MODERN PROMETHEUS
Wood engravings by Barry Moser

Barry Moser was a student of Leonard Baskin's, absorbing many of his teacher's best qualities and combining them with extraordinary finish, flourish, and skill. Moser learned much about printing from Harold McGrath, the pressman at Baskin's Gehenna Press, with whom Moser formed a partnership to print, among other things, the Pennyroyal Press books. Several notable volumes were issued, including John Walsdorf's *Men of Printing,* designed by Richard Hendel, and Lewis Carroll's *Alice in Wonderland.* But Moser's dark, precise style is perhaps best suited to Mary Shelley's *Frankenstein.* The heavy, somewhat rough-around-the-edges Poliphilus text type (set by Michael and Winifred Bixler) is a perfect choice for the book, combined with a textura display type (Wilhelm Klingsporschrift, designed by Rudolf Koch) that adds just the right gothic touch. Type and engravings were carefully printed by McGrath on specially made Strathmore paper.

93. The Janus Press (Claire Van Vliet); Newark, Vermont, 1984
CHARLES G. FINNEY · THE CIRCUS OF DR. LAO
Relief etchings by Claire Van Vliet

At her Janus Press in Vermont's Northeast Kingdom, Claire Van Vliet has combined the finest aspects of private press enterprise – careful typesetting, precise presswork – with a freshness and inventiveness rarely seen in modern fine printing. This edition of Charles Finney's *Circus of Dr. Lao* exemplifies all these qualities. The text is set in Monotype Plantin, with an unusual grotesque display font adding appropriate character. The presswork of both type and relief prints (by Van Vliet herself) is faultless; the paper is a sensuous, rough, toned paper; and the binding utilizes an unusual – yet functional and attractive – exposed sewing structure. The challenge of this book, the complexity of the typography and original prints, made it a trying production for Van Vliet, but the result is considered by many to be her masterpiece.

94. Gilman Paper Company (Richard Benson & Martino Mardersteig); Newport,
Rhode Island, 1985

PHOTOGRAPHS FROM THE COLLECTION OF THE GILMAN PAPER COMPANY

This volume displays many books notable for the extraordinary care expended in the cause of fine printing: the magnificent Trianon Press facsimile of Blake took seven years to produce; Beckmann's *Apocalypse* was published under the most trying wartime conditions; the Doves *Bible* and Bremer *De Civilitate Dei* are monumental jobs of hand composition and hand printing. Side by side with these impressive volumes stands *Photographs from the Collection of the Gilman Paper Company.* Though camera work, platemaking and printing of offset lithography are drastically different from letterpress printing of hand-set type on handmade paper, neither care nor expense was spared in striving for the most accurate reproductions possible of this collection of monuments from the history of photography. For this project, Gilman Paper bought and installed a press in Richard Benson's basement, giving him all the time he needed to produce the extraordinarily difficult facsimiles. Some "black and white" images required eight passes through the press to achieve absolute fidelity. In addition to Benson's major contribution, Meriden-Stinehour Press printed several images requiring four-color process, and Martino Mardersteig printed the text by letterpress from Monotype Bembo (metal) type. In all, it is a staggering achievement and one of the great examples of corporate sponsorship of the arts.

95. Technische Hochschule Darmstadt, Darmstadt, Germany, 1988

VARIOUS AUTHORS · MAX CAFLISCH: TYPOGRAPHIA PRACTICA

Germany's heritage of fine printing made it a leader in the field for much of the century. From Koch and Kredel through the Cranach and Bremer Presses, and on to Zapf and de Beauclair more recently, fine printing thrived in Germany for most of the century, with the notable exceptions of the two tragic world wars and their aftermaths.

Walter Wilkes at the Technische Hochschule Darmstadt has continued the tradition of fine bookmaking with excellent volumes printed by letterpress and offset at that institute of higher learning. Many of his publications deal with various aspects of both early and recent printing history. This compendium of the work of the great Swiss designer, Max Caflisch (b. 1916) is an appropriate tribute to his legacy of designing hundreds of handsome volumes for various publishers. While most of Caflisch's clients were Swiss, they also included the Imprint Society and Limited Editions Club in America. Exceptional in this volume are the more than two hundred fine reproductions, faithfully reproduced in their wide-ranging original colors.

96. Gehenna Press (Leonard Baskin); Leeds, Massachusetts, 1988

LEONARD BASKIN · ICONES LIBRORUM ARTIFICES
Etchings by Leonard Baskin

In the 1980s Leonard Baskin's Gehenna Press took a pronounced turn in a different direction. The books became more colorful, more expensive, and more "deluxe" – often the entire edition was hand bound in full leather and printed on handmade paper, with fifty copies or fewer published. Of this new genre of Gehenna books, *Icones Artifices* is surely one of the most beautiful, with thirty-two etchings of engravers, illustrators, and binders printed in various colors. According to Baskin, "*Icones* has been called the masterwork of the press It may be, I cannot say." The typesetting in Arrighi and Centaur, the presswork by Arthur Larson, and the splendid binding by Claudia Cohen with its leather onlays are especially fine.

97. Abattoir Editions (Harry Duncan); Omaha, Nebraska, 1989

CHARLES MARTIN (trans.) · THE POEMS OF CATULLUS

Harry Duncan's work in the fine printing arena spanned several decades, from his beginnings at the Cummington School in the Massachusetts hill town, though his years in the Midwest at Iowa and Nebraska. This 1989 edition edition of the *Poems of Catullus* shows the attributes for which Duncan's books were admired through a good part of the century: the types are classic yet uncommon (Eric Gill's Joanna and Van Krimpen's Romulus Open), the paper lovely (Rives Heavyweight from France), and the layout and letterpress printing clear and handsome. The quarter-linen binding with its monochrome marbled paper sides and single paper label completes one of the most beautiful examples of Duncan's bookmaking skills.

98. The Whittington Press (John & Rosalind Randle); Herefordshire, England, 1992

DAVID BUTCHER · THE STANBROOK ABBEY PRESS 1956–1990

A highlight of the exceptional publication program of the Whittington Press is their printing of many books that are of great significance in the field of printing history. Their bibliophilic journal, *Matrix,* published annually since 1981, is perhaps the most important periodical of its kind in the century, rivaled only by *The Fleuron* and *Signature.* Many full-scale books on printing-related subjects have also been printed and published at Whittington, ranging from titles on William Morris and Emery Walker to bibliographies of Saint Dominic's Press and his own Whittington Press. This 1992 book on the Stanbrook Abbey Press, an operation in an English cloistered abbey overseen by Dame Hildreth Cummings that printed not only splendid limited (and often illuminated) editions but also announcements and prayers for use in the abbey itself, is a fitting tribute to one of the most "private" presses chosen for this list. Not only are the contents of the volume encompassing, but the production itself makes it worthy of inclusion. Randle chose Van Krimpen's rare but beautiful Romulus type for the text (quite appropriate since most of the finest books of the Stanbrook Abbey Press have been printed in various Van Krimpen types). The paper is a lovely, soft, mould-made sheet from the Zerkall mill in Germany. The illustrations are particularly noteworthy in this volume: included are tritone and four-color offset reproductions, resetting in facsimile of assorted pages from their books, and original sheets from the Stanbrook Abbey Press itself.

99. I. M. Imprimit (Ian Mortimer); London, England, 1993

JAMES MOSLEY · ORNAMENTED TYPES

Ian Mortimer of I. M. Imprimit bucked the trend by continuing to print on the handpress into the closing years of the millennium. Only by that method could he bring out the full beauty of these rare examples of ornamented wood types from the holdings of the St. Bride Printing Library of London, England. The large assortment of wood type fonts is perfectly printed in this elephant folio volume – a project that took up much of the attention of both printer (Mortimer) and author (James Mosley of St. Bride's) for several years. Wood type was a nineteenth-century phenomenon, often engraved directly on boxwood by skilled craftsmen and requiring careful makeready to bring out the elaborate details. The alphabets cut by Pochée at his foundry are among the finest examples of this genre. The publication was awarded the coveted Felice Feliciano Prize in 1994.

100. Wild Carrot Letterpress; Hadley, Massachusetts
(Vincent FitzGerald & Jerry Kelly; New York, New York), 1996

JALALUDDIN MOHAMMAD RUMI (Zahra Partovi, trans.)
DIVAN-E-SHAMS
Illustrations by fifteen artists

There is a pleasant symmetry in ending these hundred selections with a beautiful *livre d'artiste,* just as they begin with Bonnard's beautiful *Parallèlement.* Just about in the middle come the monumental books by Picasso, Matisse, Beckmann, and Derain.

Vincent FitzGerald & Company of New York has issued close to fifty artists' books, this being the most challenging and complex. Since 1981 FitzGerald has been publishing selections from the *Masnavi* by the Persian mystic and poet, Jalaluddin Mohammad Rumi. For the *Divan-E-Shams,* fifteen artists were asked to illustrate this other major work by Rumi. The results are diverse, with almost as many printmaking techniques represented as artists, all held together by consistent typography in Zapf's Renaissance roman font with calligraphic title and initials by Jerry Kelly. Among the printmaking processes used here are etching, aquatint, mezzotint, collage, pochoir, chine appliqué, and computer-generated plotter imagery.

CATALOGUE

Sizes are in inches to the nearest ⅛ inch; width by height. Most illustrations have been reduced.

Place of publication is given only if it differs from place listed for designer. Publisher is listed in all cases, even when the same as the press's name.

Illustrator is listed only for certain books where the artwork is especially significant to the publication. Designer's name, if different, is noted within parentheses.

Titles are given without subtitles.

For further descriptions please see the numbers in brackets at the end of entries, which refer to the bibliography beginning on page 103.

« Elle a, ta chair, le charme sombre
Des maturités estivales,
Elle en a l'ambre, elle en a l'ombre;

« Ta voix tonne dans les rafales,
Et ta chevelure sanglante
Fuit brusquement dans la nuit lente. »

SAPPHO.

Furieuse, les yeux caves & les seins roides,
Sappho, que la langueur de son désir irrite,
Comme une louve court le long des grèves froides;

Elle songe à Phaon, oublieuse du Rite,
Et, voyant à ce point ses larmes dédaignées,
Arrache ses cheveux immenses par poignées;

Puis elle évoque, en des remords sans accalmies,
Ces temps où rayonnait, pure, la jeune gloire
De ses amours chantés en vers que la mémoire
De l'âme va redire aux vierges endormies :

19

1. L'Imprimerie Nationale (Pierre Bonnard); Paris, France
Paul Verlaine, *Parallèlement*. 9⅝ x 11⅞
Ambroise Vollard. 200 copies, Garamond Italic type. [*see bibliography no. 12*]

TITLE-PAGES

I

THE COLOPHON

O study changes of fashion in title-pages one should begin at the actual beginning, and this beginning is to be found not on the first but on the last printed leaf of the early book.

The manuscript books taken as copy by the first printers had no title-pages. When the name of the book had been fairly lettered on the outside of the cover, as was customary, there seemed no reason for its repetition inside in the form of a full page. Vellum and linen paper were then of high price, and the giving up of an entire leaf for a title-page may have been adjudged needless waste by the frugal

3   I

2. Theodore Low De Vinne; New York, New York   1901
T. L. De Vinne, *Title-Pages as Seen by a Printer.* 6½ x 9½
The Grolier Club. 325 copies, Renner type. [*see bibliography no. 3*]

 Canto Quinto.

COSI discesi del cerchio primaio
   Giù nel secondo, che men loco cinghia,
   E tanto più dolor, che pugne a guaio.
   Stavvi Minos orribilmente e ringhia:
Esamina le colpe nell' entrata,
   Giudica & manda secondo che avvinghia.
Dico, che quando l'anima mal nata
   Li vien dinanzi, tutta si confessa;
   E quel conoscitor delle peccata
Vede qual loco d'inferno è da essa:
   Cignesi colla coda tante volte
   Quantunque gradi vuol che giù sia messa.
Sempre dinanzi a lui ne stanno molte:
   Vanno a vicenda ciascuna al giudizio;
   Dicono e odono, e poi son giù volte.

30

3. Ashendene Press (C. H. St. John Hornby); Chelsea, England   1902
Dante Alighieri, *Lo Inferno.* 5½ x 7¾
Ashendene Press. Three volumes, 149 copies, Subiaco type. [*see bibliography no. 4*]

IN THE BEGINNING

GOD CREATED THE HEAVEN AND THE EARTH. ❡ AND THE EARTH WAS WITHOUT FORM, AND VOID; AND DARKNESS WAS UPON THE FACE OF THE DEEP, & THE SPIRIT OF GOD MOVED UPON THE FACE OF THE WATERS. ❡ And God said, Let there be light: & there was light. And God saw the light, that it was good: & God divided the light from the darkness. And God called the light Day, and the darkness he called Night. And the evening and the morning were the first day. ❡ And God said, Let there be a firmament in the midst of the waters, & let it divide the waters from the waters. And God made the firmament, and divided the waters which were under the firmament from the waters which were above the firmament: & it was so. And God called the firmament Heaven. And the evening & the morning were the second day. ❡ And God said, Let the waters under the heaven be gathered together unto one place, and let the dry land appear: and it was so. And God called the dry land Earth; and the gathering together of the waters called he Seas: and God saw that it was good. And God said, Let the earth bring forth grass, the herb yielding seed, and the fruit tree yielding fruit after his kind, whose seed is in itself, upon the earth: & it was so. And the earth brought forth grass, & herb yielding seed after his kind, & the tree yielding fruit, whose seed was in itself, after his kind: and God saw that it was good. And the evening & the morning were the third day. ❡ And God said, Let there be lights in the firmament of the heaven to divide the day from the night; and let them be for signs, and for seasons, and for days, & years: and let them be for lights in the firmament of the heaven to give light upon the earth: & it was so. And God made two great lights; the greater light to rule the day, and the lesser light to rule the night: he made the stars also. And God set them in the firmament of the heaven to give light upon the earth, and to rule over the day and over the night, & to divide the light from the darkness: and God saw that it was good. And the evening and the morning were the fourth day. ❡ And God said, Let the waters bring forth abundantly the moving creature that hath life, and fowl that may fly above the earth in the open firmament of heaven. And God created great whales, & every living creature that moveth, which the waters brought forth abundantly, after their kind, & every winged fowl after his kind: & God saw that it was good. And God blessed them, saying, Be fruitful, & multiply, and fill the waters in the seas, and let fowl multiply in the earth. And the evening & the morning were the fifth day. ❡ And God said, Let the earth bring forth the living creature after his kind, cattle, and creeping thing, and beast of the earth after his kind: and it was so. And God made the beast of the earth after his kind, and cattle after their kind, and every thing that creepeth upon the

27

4. Doves Press (T. J. Cobden-Sanderson); Hammersmith, England   1903–1905

The English Bible. 9¼ x 13¼

Doves Press. Five volumes. 502 copies, Doves type. [*see bibliography no. 13*]

SONGS BY BEN JONSON. A SELECTION FROM THE PLAYS, MASQUES, AND POEMS, WITH THE EARLIEST KNOWN SETTINGS OF CERTAIN NUMBERS.

THE ERAGNY PRESS, THE BROOK, HAMMERSMITH, LONDON, W.

5. The Eragny Press (Lucien and Esther Pissarro); Hammersmith, England
Ben Jonson, *Songs by Ben Jonson.* 5¼ x 8¼
The Eragny Press. 185 copies, Brook type. [*see bibliography no. 53*]

AN EPISTLE containing the strange Medical Experience of Karshish, the Arab Physician

KARSHISH, the picker-up of learning's crumbs,
The not-incurious in God's handiwork
(This man's-flesh He hath admirably made,
Blown like a bubble, kneaded like a paste,
To coop up and keep down on earth a space
That puff of vapour from His mouth, man's soul)
—To Abib, all-sagacious in our art,
Breeder in me of what poor skill I boast,
Like me inquisitive how pricks and cracks
Befall the flesh through too much stress and strain,
Whereby the wily vapour fain would slip
Back and rejoin its source before the term, —
And aptest in contrivance, under God,
To baffle it by deftly stopping such :—
The vagrant Scholar to his Sage at home
Sends greeting (health & knowledge, fame with peace)
Three samples of true snake-stone — rarer still,
One of the other sort, the melon-shaped,
(But fitter, pounded fine, for charms than drugs)
And writeth now the twenty-second time.

❡ My journeyings were brought to Jericho,
Thus I resume. Who studious in our art
Shall count a little labour unrepaid?

74

6. Doves Press (T. J. Cobden-Sanderson); Hammersmith, England   1908
Robert Browning, *Men & Women*. 6⅝ x 9¼
Doves Press. Two volumes. 262 copies, Doves type. [*see bibliography no. 13*]

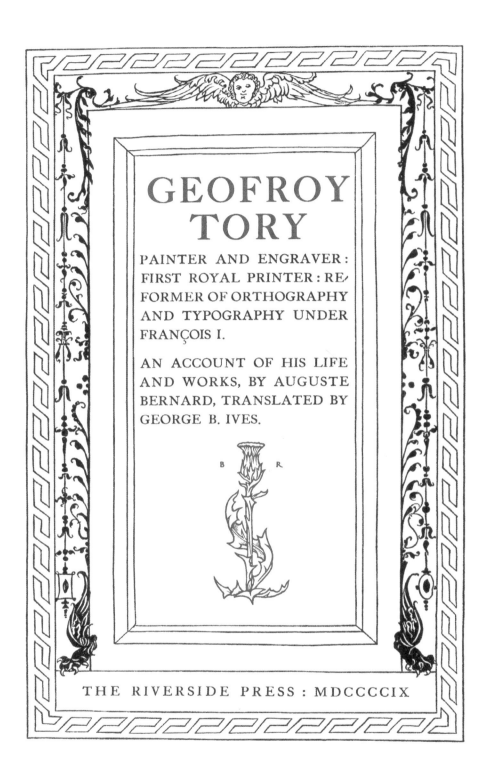

GEOFROY
TORY

PAINTER AND ENGRAVER:
FIRST ROYAL PRINTER: RE⁄
FORMER OF ORTHOGRAPHY
AND TYPOGRAPHY UNDER
FRANÇOIS I.

AN ACCOUNT OF HIS LIFE
AND WORKS, BY AUGUSTE
BERNARD, TRANSLATED BY
GEORGE B. IVES.

THE RIVERSIDE PRESS : MDCCCCIX

7. The Riverside Press (Bruce Rogers); Cambridge, Massachusetts   1909
Aurgust Bernard, *Geofroy Tory*. 7⅜ x 11⅛
Houghton Mifflin. 370 copies, Riverside Caslon type. [*see bibliography no. 54*]

EDWARD CALVERT

TEN SPIRITUAL DESIGNS

ENLARGED FROM PROOFS OF THE ORIGINALS
ON COPPER, WOOD AND STONE
MDCCCXXVII – MDCCCXXXI

PORTLAND MAINE
THOMAS BIRD MOSHER
MDCCCCXIII

8. Thomas Bird Mosher; Portland, Maine
Edward Calvert, *Ten Spiritual Designs*. 10 x 12¾
Thomas Bird Mosher. 400 copies, Old Style Roman type. [*see bibliography no. 29*]

1913

NEWARK

A SERIES OF ENGRAVINGS ON WOOD BY

RUDOLPH RUZICKA

WITH AN APPRECIATION OF
THE PICTORIAL ASPECTS OF THE TOWN
BY WALTER PRICHARD EATON

THE CARTERET BOOK CLUB
NEWARK · NEW JERSEY
1917

9. The Merrymount Press (Daniel Berkeley Updike); Boston, Massachusetts   1917
Walter Prichard Eaton, *Newark*, with wood engravings by Rudolph Ruzicka. 9¼ x 12
The Carteret Book Club. 200 copies, Caslon type. [*see bibliography no. 52*]

NOTES & JOURNAL
OF
TRAVEL IN EUROPE

═══

December 1

I HAVE been for three or four days past engaged in examining the paintings in several of the palaces. In this employment I was accompanied by a Mr Wilson — the young Scotch man whom I mentioned before as having seen at Mrs Birds. He very obligingly acted as cicerone and being acquainted with every painting of merit in Genoa he acquitted himself very well. To enter into a detail of the many fine pieces I have seen would be fatiguing. Among the finest are a *Holy Family* by Reubens in the Palace of Giacomo Balbi — Diogenes looking for an honest man — Rape of the Sabines — Perseus with Medusa's head — Jezabel devourd by dogs — all four by Luca Giordano a painter of great merit (It is one of the peculiarities of this painter that he continually changes his style in his different paintings) Magdalene with a death's head by Guido &c &c all in the same palace. In the palace of Marcellino Durazzo is an exquisite painting of

10. The Merrymount Press (Daniel Berkeley Updike); Boston, Massachusetts   1921
Washington Irving, *Notes and Journal of Travel in Europe*, with aquatints by Rudolph Ruzicka. 4¼ x 6¾
The Grolier Club. 257 copies, Oxford type. [*see bibliography no. 52*]

Canto primo.

DI COLUI che tutto move
per l'universo penetra, e risplende
in una parte più, e meno altrove.
Nel ciel che più della sua luce prende,
fu' io; e vidi cose che ridire
nè sa nè può chi di lassù discende;
Perchè, appressando sè al suo disire,
nostro intelletto si profonda tanto,
che retro la memoria non può ire.
Veramente quant'io del regno santo
nella mia mente potei far tesoro,
sarà ora materia del mio canto.
O buono Apollo, all'ultimo lavoro
fammi del tuo valor sì fatto vaso,
come domandi a dar l'amato alloro.
Infino a qui l'un giogo di Parnaso
assai mi fu; ma or con amendue
m'è uopo entrar nell'aringo rimaso.
Entra nel petto mio, e spira tue,
sì come quando Marsia traesti
della vagina delle membra sue.
310

11. Bremer Presse; Munich, Germany   1921
Dante Alighieri, *La Divina Commedia*. 8¼ x 13¼
Bremer Presse. 300 copies, Bremer Roman type. [*see bibliography no. 37*]

ἴϲον τείνειεν πολέμου τέλοϲ, οὔ κε μάλα ῥέα
νικήϲει, οὐδ᾽ εἰ παγχάλκεοϲ εὔχεται εἶναι.
Τὸν δ᾽ αὖτε προϲέειπε ἄναξ Διὸϲ υἱὸϲ Ἀπόλλων·
Ἥρωϲ, ἀλλ᾽ ἄγε καὶ ϲὺ θεοῖϲ᾽ αἰειγενέτῃϲιν
εὔχεο· καὶ δὲ ϲέ φαϲι Διὸϲ κούρηϲ Ἀφροδίτηϲ
ἐκγεγάμεν, κεῖνοϲ δὲ χερείονοϲ ἐκ θεοῦ ἐϲτιν.
ἣ μὲν γὰρ Διόϲ ἐϲθ᾽, ἣ δ᾽ ἐξ ἁλίοιο γέροντοϲ.
ἀλλ᾽ ἰθὺϲ φέρε χαλκὸν ἀτειρέα, μηδέ ϲε πάμπαν
λευγαλέοιϲι ἔπεϲϲιν ἀποτρεπέτω καὶ ἀρειῇ.
Ὣϲ εἰπὼν ἔμπνευϲε μένοϲ μέγα ποιμένι λαῶν,
βῆ δὲ διὰ προμάχων κεκορυθμένοϲ αἴθοπι χαλκῶι.
οὐδ᾽ ἔλαθ᾽ Ἀγχίϲαο πάιϲ λευκώλενον Ἥρην
ἀντία Πηλείωνοϲ ἰὼν ἀνὰ οὐλαμὸν ἀνδρῶν,
ἣ δ᾽ ἄμυδιϲ ϲτήϲαϲα θεοὺϲ μετὰ μῦθον ἔειπεν·
Φράζεϲθον δὴ ϲφῶι, Ποϲείδαον καὶ Ἀθήνη,
ἐν φρεϲὶν ὑμετέρῃϲιν ὅπωϲ ἔϲται τάδε ἔργα.
Αἰνείαϲ ὅδ᾽ ἔβη κεκορυθμένοϲ αἴθοπι χαλκῶι
ἀντία Πηλείωνοϲ, ἀνῆκε δὲ Φοῖβοϲ Ἀπόλλων.
ἀλλ᾽ ἄγεθ᾽, ἡμεῖϲ πέρ μιν ἀποτροπόωμεν ὀπίϲϲω
αὐτόθεν ἤ τιϲ ἔπειτα καὶ ἡμείων Ἀχιλῆι
παρϲταίη, δοίη δὲ κράτοϲ μέγα, μηδέ τι θυμοῦ
δευέϲθω, ἵνα εἴδει ὅ μιν φιλέουϲιν ἄριϲτοι
ἀθανάτων, οἳ δ᾽ αὖτ᾽ ἀνεμώλιοι οἳ τὸ πάροϲ περ
Τρωϲὶν ἀμύνουϲιν πόλεμον καὶ δηιοτῆτα.
πάντεϲ δ᾽ Οὐλύμποιο κατήλθομεν ἀντιόωντεϲ
τῆϲδε μάχηϲ, ἵνα μή τι μετὰ Τρώεϲϲι πάθῃϲι,
ϲήμερον, ὕϲτερον αὖτε τὰ πείϲεται ἄϲϲα οἱ αἶϲα
γεινομένωι ἐπένηϲε λίνωι, ὅτε μιν τέκε μήτηρ.
εἰ δ᾽ Ἀχιλεὺϲ οὐ ταῦτα θεῶν ἐκ πεύϲεται ὀμφῆϲ,
δείϲετ᾽ ἔπειθ᾽, ὅτε κέν τιϲ ἐναντίβιον θεὸϲ ἔλθῃ
ἐν πολέμωι, χαλεποὶ δὲ θεοὶ φαίνεϲθαι ἐναργεῖϲ.
Τὴν δ᾽ ἠμείβετ᾽ ἔπειτα Ποϲειδάων ἐνοίχθων·
Ἥρη, μὴ χαλέπαινε παρὲκ νόον, οὐδέ τί ϲε χρή.
οὐκ ἂν ἐγώ γ᾽ ἐθέλοιμι θεοὺϲ ἔριδι ξυνελάϲϲαι

Υ 101-134

12. Bremer Presse; Munich, Germany   1923–24
Homer, *Iliad* and *Odyssey*. 8⅞ x 13¾
Bremer Presse. Two volumes. 615 copies, Bremer Greek type. [*see bibliography no. 37*]

WACHE

Indessen dass der Corso immer belebter wird, und unter den vielen Personen, die in ihren gewöhnlichen Kleidern spazieren, sich hier und da ein Pulcinell zeigt, hat sich das Militär vor der Porta del Popolo versammelt. Es zieht, angeführt von dem General zu Pferde, in guter Ordnung und neuer Montur mit klingendem Spiel den Corso herauf und besetzt sogleich alle Eingänge in denselben, errichtet ein paar Wachen auf den Hauptplätzen und übernimmt die Sorge für die Ordnung der ganzen Anstalt.

Die Verleiher der Stühle und Gerüste rufen nun emsig den Vorbeigehenden an: Luoghi! Luoghi, Padroni! Luoghi!

MASKEN

Nun fangen die Masken an sich zu vermehren. Junge Männer, geputzt in Festtagskleidern der Weiber aus der untersten Classe, mit entblösstem Busen und frecher Selbstgenügsamkeit, lassen

19

13. Officina Bodoni (Giovanni Mardersteig); Montagnola di Lugano, Switzerland   1924
Johann Wolfgang von Goethe, *Das Roemische Carneval 1788*. 8¼ x 12
Editiones Officinae Bodoni. 230 copies, Bodoni Cancelleresco type. [*see bibliography no. 39*]

S·AVRELII AVGVSTINI DE CIVITATE DEI LIBRI XXII

14. Bremer Presse; Munich, Germany

1925

S. Aurelii Augustini, *De Civitate Dei*. 9¾ x 13¾

Bremer Presse. 385 copies, Bremer Roman type. [*see bibliography no. 37*]

P. VERGILI MARONIS ECLOGA QUARTA
POLLIO

SICELIDES MUSAE, PAULO MAIORA
CANAMUS!
NON OMNIS ARBUSTA IUVANT
HUMILISQUE MYRICAE:
SI CANIMUS SILVAS, SILVAE SINT
CONSULE DIGNAE.

ULTIMA CUMAEI VENIT IAM
CARMINIS AETAS;
MAGNUS AB INTEGRO
SAECLORUM NASCITUR ORDO.
IAM REDIT ET VIRGO, REDEUNT
SATURNIA REGNA;
IAM NOVA PROGENIES CAELO
DEMITTITUR ALTO.

36

15. Cranach Presse; Weimar, Germany   1926

Virgil, *The Eclogues of Virgil*, with woodcuts by Aristide Maillol. 10 x 12⅞

Cranach Presse. English edition: 266 copies, Cranach Roman type. [*see bibliography no. 42*]

DAS EVANGELIUM MATTHÄUS +

1 Dies ist das Buch von der Geburt Jesu Christi,
der da ist ein Sohn Davids, des Sohnes Abra=
2 hams. Abraham zeugte Isaak. Isaak zeugte Ja=
3 kob. Jakob zeugte Juda und seine Brüder. Juda
zeugte Perez und Serah von der Thamar. Perez
4 zeugte hezron. hezron zeugte Ram. Ram zeug=
te Amminadab. Amminadab zeugte Nahesson.
5 Nahesson zeugte Salma. Salma zeugte Boas von
der Rahab. Boas zeugte Obed von der Ruth.
6 Obed zeugte Jesse. Jesse zeugte den König Da=
vid. Der König David zeugte Salomo von dem
7 Weib des Uria. Salomo zeugte Rehabeam. Re=
8 habeam zeugte Abia. Abia zeugte Asa. Asa
zeugte Josaphat. Josaphat zeugte Joram. Jo=
9 ram zeugte Usia. Usia zeugte Jotham. Jotham
10 zeugte Ahas. Ahas zeugte hiskia. hiskia zeug=
te Manasse. Manasse zeugte Amon. Amon zeug=
11 te Josia. Josia zeugte Jechonja und seine Brüder
um die Zeit der babylonischen Gefangenschaft.

3

16. Gebr. Klingspor (Rudolf Koch); Offenbach am Main, Germany   1926
Die Vier Evangelien. 4¾ x 6½
Rudolf Koch. 800 copies, Peter Jessen-Schrift type. [*see bibliography no. 24*]

A DISTINGUISHED FAMILY OF
FRENCH PRINTERS OF THE
SIXTEENTH CENTURY
HENRI & ROBERT
ESTIENNE

London:
Linotype & Machinery Ltd., 9 Kingsway
1929

17. "The Sign of the Dolphin" (George W. Jones); London, England   1929
A Distinguished Family of French Printers of the Sixteenth Century: Henri & Robert Estienne. 8½ x 13¼
Linotype & Machinery Company. 400 copies, Estienne Old Face type. [*see bibliography no. 46*]

INFERNO

THE COMEDY OF DANTE ALIGHIERI OF FLORENCE
COMMONLY CALLED THE DIVINE COMEDY
A LINE-FOR-LINE TRANSLATION IN THE RIME-FORM OF
THE ORIGINAL BY
MELVILLE BEST ANDERSON

SAN FRANCISCO
PRINTED BY JOHN HENRY NASH
MCMXXIX

18. John Henry Nash; San Francisco, California

1929

Dante Alighieri, *The Divine Comedy.* 9 x 14
John Henry Nash. Four volumes. 250 copies, Cloister Light type. [*see bibliography no. 27*]

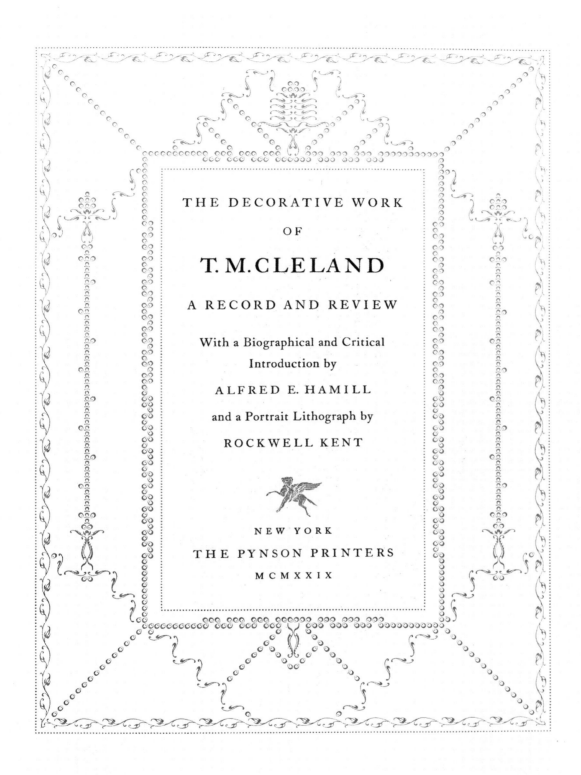

THE DECORATIVE WORK

OF

T. M. CLELAND

A RECORD AND REVIEW

With a Biographical and Critical
Introduction by

ALFRED E. HAMILL

and a Portrait Lithograph by

ROCKWELL KENT

NEW YORK
THE PYNSON PRINTERS
MCMXXIX

19. The Pynson Printers (Elmer Adler); New York, New York

Alfred E. Hamill (Introduction), *The Decorative Work of T. M. Cleland*. 9¼ x 12¼

The Pynson Printers. 1,200 copies, Caslon type. [*see bibliography no. 15*]

1929

76   Diptam

20. Mainzer Presse (Rudolf Koch and Fritz Kredel); Mainz, Germany   1929–30
Rudolf Koch, *Das Blumenbuch*. 9 x 12½
Insel Verlag. Three volumes. 1,000 copies, Peter Jessen-Schrift type. [*see bibliography no. 24*]

sureux, laquelle il cloua par le pa-
vé de la sale, qui estoit tout d'aiz
et aux coingz il mist les tisons
qu'il avoit aguisez, et desquels
a esté parlé cy dessus, qui ser-
voyent d'attaches, les liant avec
telle façon, que quelque effort
qu'ils feissent, il leur fut impos-
sible de se despestrer, et soudain
il mit le feu par les quatre coings
de la maison Royalle: de sorte que
de ceux qui estoyent en la sale,
il n'en eschappa pas un seul, qui
ne purgeast ses fautes par le
feu, et ne dessechast le trop de li-
gueur qu'il avoit avallee, mourans
trestous enveloppez dans l'ar-
deur inevitable des flammes. Ce
que voyant l'Adolescent, devenu
sage, et sachant que son oncle s'e-
stoit retiré avant la fin du banquet,
en son corps de logis, separé du
lieu exposé aux flammes, s'en y
alla, si que entrant en sa chambre,
se saisit de l'espee du meurtrier
de son pere, et y laissa la sienne au
lieu, qu'on luy avoit clouee avec
le fourreau, durant le banquet:
puis s'adressant à Fengon, luy
dist: Je m'estonne, Roy desloyal,
comme tu dors ainsi à ton aise,
tandis que ton Palais est tout en
feu, et que l'embrasement d'ice-
luy a bruslé tous les courtisans,
et ministres de tes cruautez, et de-
testables tyrannies: et ne sçais
comme tu es si asseuré de ta for-
tune, que de reposer, voyant Amleth si pres de toy, et armé des
pieux qu'il aiguisa, il y a long
temps, et qui à present est tout
prest de se venger du tort, et inju-
re traistresse par toy faite à son
seigneur et pere. Fengon cognois-
sant à la verité la descouverte des
ruses de son nepveu, et l'oyant
parler de sens rassis, et qui plus
est, luy voyant le glaive nud en
main, que desja il bauçoit pour le priver de vie, sauta legerement du lict, jettant la main à l'espee
clouee de son nepveu, laquelle comme il s'efforçoit de desgaigner, Amleth luy donna un grand
coup sur le chinon du col, de sorte qu'il luy feit voler la teste par terre, disant: c'est le salaire deu
à ceux qui te ressemblent, que de mourir ainsi violemment: et pour ce va, et estant aux enfers, ne
faux de compter à ton frere, que tu occis meschamment, que c'est son fils qui te faict faire ce mes-
sage, à fin que soulagé par ceste memoire, son ombre s'appaise parmy les esprits bien heureux,
et me quitte de celle obligation qui m'astraignoit à poursuivre ceste vengeance sur mon sang

Estrange vengeance prise par Amleth.

Mocquerie poignante d'Amleth à son oncle.

Fengon occis par Amleth son nepveu.

Ophe. (shee sings)
　How should I pour true love know
　From another one,
　By his cockle hat and staffe,
　And his Sendall shoone.
Queene. Alas sweet Lady, what imports this song?

124

21. Cranach Presse; Weimar, Germany　　　　　　　　　　　　　　　　　　1929–30
William Shakespeare, *The Tragedie of Hamlet,* with woodcuts by Edward Gordon-Craig. 9⅛ x 13¾
Cranach Presse. 325 copies, Hamlet-Fraktur type. [*see bibliography no. 42*]

CHAPTER XCIX   THE DOUBLOON

ERE now it has been related how Ahab was wont to pace his quarter-deck, taking regular turns at either limit, the binnacle and main-mast; but in the multiplicity of other things requiring narration it has not been added how that sometimes in these walks, when most plunged in his mood, he was wont to pause in turn at each spot, and stand there strangely eyeing the particular object before him. When he halted before the binnacle, with his glance fastened on the pointed needle in the compass, that glance shot like a javelin with the pointed intensity of his purpose; and when resuming his walk he again paused before the main-mast, then, as the same riveted glance fastened upon the riveted gold coin there, he still wore the same aspect of nailed firmness, only dashed with a certain wild longing, if not hopefulness.

But one morning, turning to pass the doubloon, he seemed to be newly attracted by the strange figures and inscriptions stamped on it, as though now for the first time beginning to interpret for himself in some monomaniac way whatever significance might lurk in them. And some certain significance lurks in all

<— 72 —>

22. The Lakeside Press; Chicago, Illinois   1930
Herman Melville, *Moby-Dick*, with wood engravings by Rockwell Kent. 8¼ x 11½
R. R. Donnelley & Sons. Three volumes. 1,000 copies, Caslon Old Style type. [*see bibliography no. 36*]

LEAVES OF GRASS

COMPRISING ALL THE POEMS WRITTEN

BY WALT WHITMAN

FOLLOWING THE ARRANGEMENT

OF THE EDITION OF

1891-'2

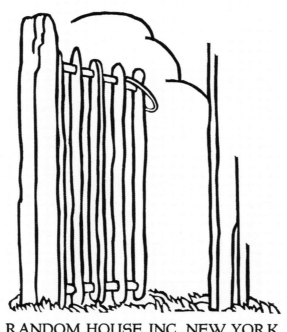

RANDOM HOUSE, INC., NEW YORK

1930

23. The Grabhorn Press; San Francisco, California
Walt Whitman, *Leaves of Grass*, with woodcuts by Valenti Angelo. 9¾ x 14½
Random House. 400 copies, Goudy Newstyle type. [*see bibliography no. 37*]

JOHN  BELL

BOOKSELLER & PART-PROPRIETOR IN
THE MORNING POST, ETC.

The career of John Bell as a bookseller seems to have opened before he was twenty-four years of age, and as a newspaper-proprietor before he was twenty-seven. The earliest indication of his activities which I have been able to find is his receipt "for Four Pounds in full for one half of my 16th share of Francis's Horace bought at Millar's Sale." The receipt is dated Sept. 13, 1769. An early imprint, "Printed for John Bell in the Strand," figures in Kenrick's *Free Thoughts on Seduction*. In 1772 he published *The Universal Catalogue*,"printed for the proprietors and sold by J. Bell near Exeter 'Change in the Strand," an octavo chronicle of current literature compiled from the *Critical Review* and the *Monthly Review*. Lengthy notices from these are appended to the title, author's name, date and place of publication. The compilation is important in the history of Catalogues and valuable as an Index to Current Literature. It is characteristic of Bell that he

1   ɪ

24. Cambridge University Press; Cambridge, England   1930
Stanley Morison, *John Bell*. 6¼ x 9¾
Cambridge University Press. 300 copies, Bell type. [*see bibliography no. 2*]

THE BOOK OF
COMMON PRAYER

and Administration of the Sacraments
and Other Rites and Ceremonies
of the Church

ACCORDING TO THE USE OF THE
PROTESTANT EPISCOPAL CHURCH
IN THE UNITED STATES OF AMERICA

Together with The Psalter
or Psalms of David

PRINTED FOR THE COMMISSION

A. D. MDCCCCXXVIII

25. The Merrymount Press (Daniel Berkeley Updike); Boston, Massachusetts   1930
The Book of Common Prayer. 9½ x 13½
Printed for the Commission. 512 copies, Janson type. [*see bibliography no. 52*]

JESUS BEING
FULL OF THE HOLY
GHOST RETURNED
FROM JORDAN, AND WAS
LED BY THE SPIRIT INTO THE
WILDERNESS, BEING FORTY
DAYS TEMPTED OF THE DEVIL. AND IN THOSE
days he did eat nothing: & when they were ended, he afterward hungered. And the devil said unto him, If thou be the Son of God, command this stone that it be made bread. And Jesus answered him, saying, It is written, That man shall not live by bread alone, but by every word of God. And the devil, taking him up into an high mountain, shewed unto him all the kingdoms of the world in a moment of time. And the devil said unto him, All this power will I give thee, and the glory of them: for that is delivered unto me; and to whomsoever I will I give it. If thou therefore wilt worship me, all shall be thine. And Jesus answered and said unto him, Get thee behind me, Satan: for it is written, Thou shalt worship the Lord thy God, and him only shalt thou serve. And he brought him to Jerusalem, and set him on a pinnacle of the temple, and said unto him, If thou be the Son of God, cast thyself down from hence: For it is written,

145

26. The Golden Cockerel Press; Waltham Saint Lawrence, England   1931
The Four Gospels of Lord Jesus Christ, with wood engravings by Eric Gill. 9¼ x 13⅛
The Golden Cockerel Press. 502 copies, Golden Cockerel type. [*see bibliography no. 23*]

AND now proud Sparta with their wheels resounds,
Sparta whose walls a range of hills surrounds:
At the fair dome the rapid labour ends;
Where sate Atrides 'midst his bridal friends,
With double vows invoking Hymen's power,
To bless his son's and daughter's nuptial hour.
  That day, to great Achilles' son resign'd,
Hermione, the fairest of her kind,
Was sent to crown the long-protracted joy,
Espoused before the final doom of Troy:
With steeds and gilded cars, a gorgeous train
Attend the nymphs to Phthia's distant reign.
Meanwhile at home, to Megapenthes' bed
The virgin-choir Alector's daughter led.
Brave Megapenthes from a stolen amour
To great Atrides' age his handmaid bore:
To Helen's bed the gods alone assign
Hermione, to extend the regal line;
On whom a radiant pomp of Graces wait,
Resembling Venus in attractive state.
  While this gay friendly troop the king surround,
With festival and mirth the roofs resound:
A bard amid the joyous circle sings
High airs, attemper'd to the vocal strings;
Whilst, warbling to the varied strain, advance

67

27. Joh. Enschedé en Zonen (Jan van Krimpen); Haarlem, The Netherlands
Homer, *The Iliad* and *The Odyssey* (Alexander Pope, trans.). 7¾ x 12
The Limited Editions Club. 1,500 copies, Romanée type. [*see bibliography no.* 17]

1931

reminiscent of the cursive handwriting from which 65
they are derived. Fig. 25 shows the three alphabets
with their customary as well as their essential differences. ¶ Properly speaking there is no such thing
as an alphabet of Italic Capitals, and where upright
or nearly upright Italics are used ordinary upright

(Figure 25 shows the Capitals, Roman Lower-case
and Italics with their customary as well as their essential differences.)

Roman Capitals go perfectly well with them. But as
Italics are commonly made with a considerable
slope & cursive freedom, various sorts of sloping &
e

28. Hague & Gill (Eric Gill and René Hague); Pigotts, England   1931
An Essay on Typography. 5 x 7¾
Sheed and Ward. 500 copies, Joanna type. [*see bibliography no. 23*]

CANTICUM CANTICORUM

4

QUOD EST SALOMONIS
SPONSA

SCULETUR ME
OSCULO ORIS SUI
QUIA MELIORA SUNT
UBERA TUA VINO,
FRAGRANTIA
UNGUENTIS OPTIMIS.
Oleum effusum nomen tuum;
ideo adolescentulae dilexerunt te.
Trahe me, post te curremus
in odorem unguentorum tuorum.
Introduxit me rex in cellaria sua;
exultabimus et laetabimur in te,
memores uberum tuorum super vinum.
Recti diligunt te.

NIGRA sum, sed formosa,
filiae Jerusalem,
sicut tabernacula Cedar,
sicut pelles Salomonis.
Nolite me considerare quod fusca sim,
quia decoloravit me sol.
Filii matris meae pugnaverunt contra me;
posuerunt me custodem in vineis,
vineam meam non custodivi.

Indica mihi, quem diligit anima mea,
ubi pascas, ubi cubes in meridie,

5

29. Cranach Presse; Weimar, Germany   1931
Canticum Canticorum Salomonis, with wood engravings by Eric Gill. 5⅛ x 10⅛
Cranach Presse. 268 copies, Jensen Antiqua type. [*see bibliography no. 42*]

For since they were so methodicall in the constitutions of their temples, as to observe the due situation, aspect, manner, form, and order in Architectonicall relations, whether they were not as distinct in their groves and Plantations about them, in form and *species* respectively unto their Deities, is not without probability of conjecture. And in their groves of the Sunne this was a fit number, by multiplication to denote the dayes of the year; and might Hieroglyphically speak as much, as the mysticall *Statua* of [1] *Janus* in the Language of his fingers. And since they were so criticall in the number of his horses, the strings of his Harp, and rayes about his head, denoting the orbes of heaven, the Seasons and Moneths of the Yeare; witty Idolatry would hardly be flat in other appropriations.

[1] Which King *Numa* set up with his fingers so disposed that they numerically denoted 365. *Pliny.*

30. Curwen Press; London, England   1932
Sir Thomas Browne, *Urne Buriall and the Garden of Cyrus*, with illustrations by Paul Nash. 9 x 12
Curwen Press. 215 copies, Bembo type. [*see bibliography no. 48*]

LIBER I

~ IX ~

Militat omnis amans, et habet sua castra Cupido:
    Attice, crede mihi, militat omnis amans.
Quae bellost habilis, Veneri quoque convenit aetas:
    Turpe senex miles, turpe senilis amor;
Quos petiere duces animos in milite forti,
    Hos petit in socio bella puella viro;
Pervigilant ambo; terra requiescit uterque:
    Ille fores dominae servat, at ille ducis;
Militis officium longast via: mitte puellam,
    Strenuus exempto fine sequetur amans;
Ibit in adversos montes duplicataque nimbo
    Flumina, congestas exteret ille nives,
Nec freta pressurus tumidos causabitur Euros
    Aptaque verrendis sidera quaeret aquis.
Quis nisi vel miles vel amans et frigora noctis
    Et denso mixtas perferet imbre nives?
Mittitur infestos alter speculator in hostes,
    In rivale oculos alter, ut hoste, tenet.
Ille graves urbes, hic durae limen amicae
    Obsidet; hic portas frangit, at ille fores.

(33)

31. Officina Bodoni (Giovanni Mardersteig); Verona, Italy   1932
P. Ovidii Nasonis, *Amores*. 6 x 9½
Editiones Officinae Bodoni. 123 copies, Arrighi-Vicenza type. [*see bibliography no. 39*]

BOOK XII

From Ocean's pouring stream our ship measured the open rolling seas even to Æaea, the isle of sunrise where Dawn the fore-runner has her house and dancing-floor: there we grounded the ship among the sand-banks and went out upon the beach, to sleep and wait for day. When the light came I sent a party up to Circe's house to bring down dead Elpenor's body. We hewed logs and built his pyre upon the tallest headland where it runs out above the sea: duly we made his funeral, bewailing him with bitter tears. After body and armour were quite burned away we piled a mound over them, and to crown it dragged up a monolith, on top of which we fixed his goodly oar. The busy work was scarcely done when Circe came, decked to receive us: our departure from Hades had not been hidden from her.

32. Bruce Rogers & Emery Walker; London, England   1932
The Odyssey of Homer (T. E. Shaw, trans.). 8 x 11½
Sir Emery Walker, Wilfred Merton, and Bruce Rogers. 530 copies, Centaur type. [*see bibliography no. 25*]

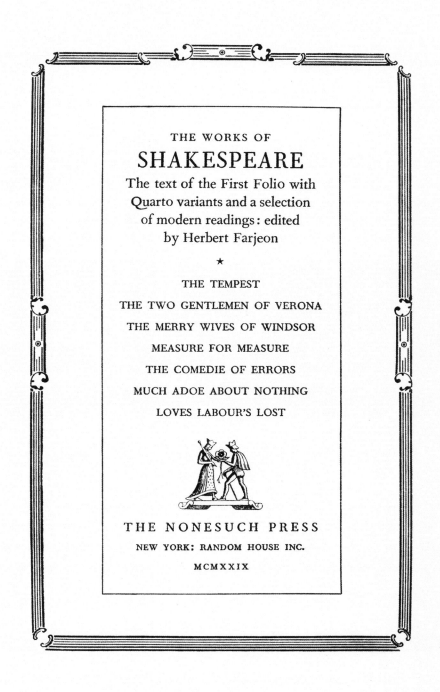

33. The Nonesuch Press (Francis Meynell); London, England   1933

William Shakespeare, *The Works of Shakespeare*. 5¾ x 9¼

The Nonesuch Press. Seven volumes. 1,050 copies, Random House, 550 copies, Fournier type. [*see bibliography no. 16*]

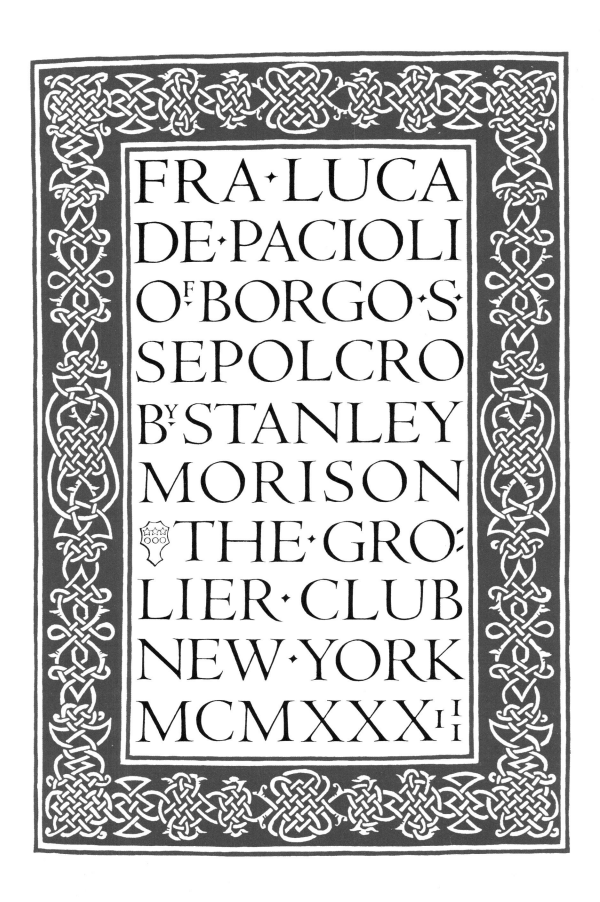

34. Cambridge University Press (Bruce Rogers); Cambridge, England 1933
Stanley Morison, *Fra Luca de Pacioli*. 8⅜ x 12⅜
The Grolier Club, New York. 390 copies, Centaur type. [*see bibliography no. 25*]

MORE THAN THIRTY-EIGHT YEARS have gone by since the Ashendene Press had its humble beginning in the little garden-house of happy memory shewn in the woodcut which heads this page. Now that its working days are drawing to a close it seems fitting that I should preface this 'Catalogue Raisonné' with a short account of its origin and, to others than myself, uneventful history. I do so in the hope that details unimportant in themselves may possibly have some interest for book-collectors and students of typography in days to come. The output of the Press, measured in relation to the years of its life, is small in amount compared with that of the Kelmscott and Doves Presses; but it must always be borne in mind that it has been the hobby of my leisure hours, that it was for many years worked entirely, except for some little help from my brother and sisters, by my own hands; and that it has never at any one time employed more than a single Pressman and a single Compositor. The fact that it has been the absorbing interest of an otherwise busy life must be pleaded as my excuse for this necessarily somewhat egotistical Foreword.

b   1

35. Ashendene Press (C. H. St. John Hornby); Chelsea, England   1935
A Descriptive Bibliography of the Books Printed at the Ashendene Press MDCCCXCV–MCMXXXV. 9 x 13
Ashendene Press. 390 copies, Ptolemy Great Primer type. [*see bibliography no. 4*]

Jan Tschichold:

Typographische Gestaltung

Benno Schwabe & Co . Basel 1935

36. Benno Schwabe & Co. (Jan Tschichold); Basel, Switzerland   1935
Typographische Gestaltung. 5¾ x 8¼
Benno Schwabe & Co. No limitation given, Bodoni type. [*see bibliography no. 35*]

THE BOOK OF PSALMS

PSALM 1

BLESSED is the man that walketh not
in the counsel of the ungodly,
Nor standeth in the way of sinners,
Nor sitteth in the seat of the scornful.
¶2 But his delight is in the law of the
LORD;
And in his law doth he meditate day and night.
¶3 And he shall be like a tree planted by the
rivers of water,
That bringeth forth his fruit in his season;
His leaf also shall not wither;
And whatsoever he doeth shall prosper.
¶4 The ungodly are not so:
But are like the chaff which the wind driveth
away.
¶5 Therefore the ungodly shall not stand in the
judgment,
Nor sinners in the congregation of the righteous.
¶6 For the LORD knoweth the way of the
righteous:
But the way of the ungodly shall perish.

PSALM 2

WHY do the heathen rage,
And the people imagine a vain thing?
¶2 The kings of the earth set them-
selves,
And the rulers take counsel together,
Against the LORD, and against his anointed, saying,
¶3 Let us break their bands asunder,
And cast away their cords from us.
¶4 He that sitteth in the heavens shall laugh:
The Lord shall have them in derision.
¶5 Then shall he speak unto them in his wrath,
And vex them in his sore displeasure.
¶6 Yet have I set my king
Upon my holy hill of Zion.
¶7 I will declare the decree:
The LORD hath said unto me, Thou art my Son;
This day have I begotten thee.
¶8 Ask of me, and I shall give thee the heathen
for thine inheritance,
And the uttermost parts of the earth for thy
possession.

472

¶9 Thou shalt break them with a rod of iron;
Thou shalt dash them in pieces like a potter's
vessel.
¶10 Be wise now therefore, O ye kings:
Be instructed, ye judges of the earth.
¶11 Serve the LORD with fear,
And rejoice with trembling.
¶12 Kiss the Son, lest he be angry, and ye perish
from the way,
When his wrath is kindled but a little.
Blessed are all they that put their trust in him.

PSALM 3

A Psalm of David, when he fled from Absalom his son.

LORD, how are they increased that trouble me!
Many are they that rise up against me.
¶2 Many there be which say of my soul,
There is no help for him in God.   Selah.
¶3 But thou, O LORD, art a shield for me;
My glory, and the lifter up of mine head.
¶4 I cried unto the LORD with my voice,
And he heard me out of his holy hill.   Selah.
¶5 I laid me down and slept;
I awaked; for the LORD sustained me.
¶6 I will not be afraid of ten thousands of
people,
That have set themselves against me round
about.
¶7 Arise, O LORD; save me, O my God:
For thou hast smitten all mine enemies upon
the cheek bone;
Thou hast broken the teeth of the ungodly.
¶8 Salvation belongeth unto the LORD:
Thy blessing is upon thy people.   Selah.

PSALM 4

To the chief Musician on Neginoth, A Psalm of David.

HEAR me when I call, O God of my
righteousness:
Thou hast enlarged me when I was in
distress;
Have mercy upon me, and hear my prayer.
¶2 O ye sons of men, how long will ye turn
my glory into shame?
How long will ye love vanity, and seek after
leasing?   Selah.

37. Oxford University Press (Bruce Rogers); Oxford, England   1935
The Holy Bible. 12¼ x 17¾
Oxford University Press. Two volumes. 200 copies, Centaur type. [*see bibliography no. 50*]

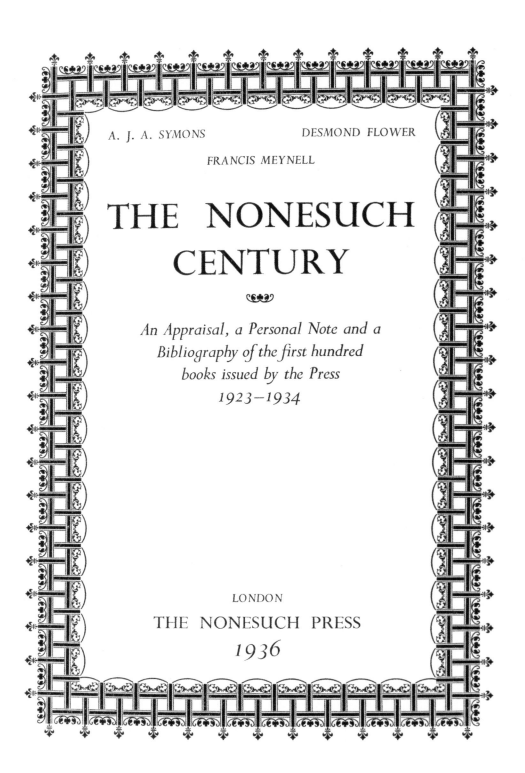

A. J. A. SYMONS   DESMOND FLOWER

FRANCIS MEYNELL

THE NONESUCH CENTURY

An Appraisal, a Personal Note and a
Bibliography of the first hundred
books issued by the Press
1923–1934

LONDON
THE NONESUCH PRESS
1936

38. The Nonesuch Press (Francis Meynell); London, England   1936
A. J. A. Symons, Desmond Flower, Francis Meynell, *The Nonesuch Century*. 7½ x 12
The Nonesuch Press. 750 copies, Times New Roman type. [*see bibliography no. 16*]

Diggings

from many ampersandhogs

39. Various printers; various places   1936
Diggings from many ampersandhogs. 3⅝ x 5⅞
The Typophiles, New York. 125 copies, various types. [*see bibliography no. 44*]

IN THE NAME OF ALMIGHTY GOD

HAVE WE ERE THIS WRITTEN A PART OF THE FAIR SAYINGS AND GOOD PRECEPTS OF OUR SAINTLY KING LOUIS THAT THOSE THAT HEAR THEM MAY FIND THEM SET ONE BESIDE THE OTHER, WHERE‑FOR THEY MAY HAVE GREATER PROFIT FROM THEM THAN AS IF THEY HAD BEEN WRITTEN AMONG HIS DEEDS. AND HEREAFTER WE ENTER UPON HIS DEEDS, IN THE NAME OF GOD AND IN HIS NAME.

April 25 1214

AS I have heard say he was born on St. Mark's Day after Easter. That day they bear crosses in procession in many parts, and in France they call them the black crosses: so that this was as it were a prophecy of the great plenty of the people that were to die in these two Crusades, that is to say in that of Egypt, and in that other on which he died at Carthage; wherefor was there much heavy grief in this world, and much great joy is there in Paradise for those who died on these two pilgrimages bearing the true cross.

November 29 1226

He was crowned on the first Sunday of Advent. On this Sunday the Mass beginneth *Ad te levavi animam meam*, and what followeth sayeth thus: 'Fair Lord God, I will lift up my soul unto Thee and in Thee is my trust.' In God did he put his trust from his childhood to his death; for as he lay dying, in his last words he called upon God and the saints and especially my Lord Saint James and my Lady Saint Genevieve.

II

GOD, in Whom he put his trust, guarded him always from his child‑hood until the end; and especially did He defend him when he was a child and there was great need of it, as ye shall hear tell hereafter. As to his soul, God kept it through the good precepts of his mother, who taught him to have faith in God and to love Him, and drew round him all manner of religious. And she made him, child as he was, say all his Hours, and go to hear sermons on feast days. He recalled that his mother had many a time given him to understand that she had liefer that he were dead than that he had done mortal sin.

20

40. The Gregynog Press; Newton, Wales   1937
John, Lord of Joinville, *The History of Saint Louis.* 9¼ x 13½
The Gregynog Press. 200 copies, Poliphilus type. [*see bibliography no. 28*]

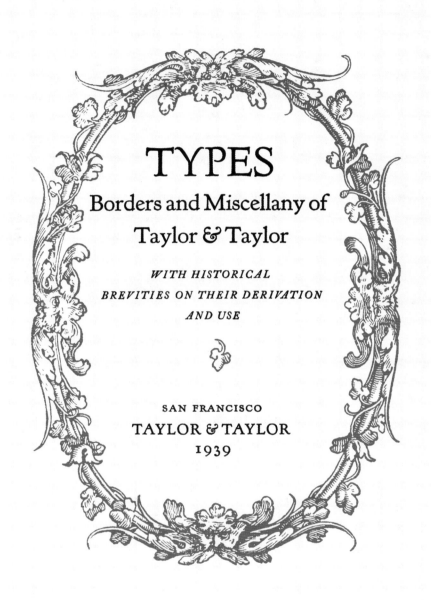

TYPES
Borders and Miscellany of
Taylor & Taylor

WITH HISTORICAL
BREVITIES ON THEIR DERIVATION
AND USE

SAN FRANCISCO
TAYLOR & TAYLOR
1939

41. Taylor & Taylor; San Francisco, California   1939
Types Borders and Miscellany of Taylor & Taylor. 6¼ x 8¾
Taylor & Taylor. 330 copies, Kennerley type. [*see bibliography no. 15*]

92. SALOME | A TRAGEDY IN ONE ACT BY OSCAR
WILDE [caption title]

10¼ x 7¾. One blank leaf; frontispiece; pp. (1⁄42); one blank leaf: consisting
of text pp. (1⁄42), colophon on last page of text.

℃ Caption title and running heads on each page printed in blue and red; de⁄
scription of scene and colophon in red. Colored frontispiece and forty⁄two col⁄
ored marginal decorations from woodblocks designed and cut by Valenti An⁄
gelo. Type Monotype Sans Serif; paper Van Gelder. Bound in parchment
decorated in gold and red; blue cloth back; title in gold on back. One hundred
and ninety⁄five copies printed for direct sale in March, 1927. Price $20.00.

℃ "Occasioned by H. L. Bullen's remark that American printing lacked color
and was too dignified."—Grabhorn.

93. THE | GOLDEN TOUCH | BY | NATHANIEL | HAW⁄
THORNE | [printer's device L] | THE GRABHORN PRESS |
MCMXXVII

9 x 5⅝. Two blank leaves; pp. (i⁄ii); pp. 1⁄36; colophon; two blank leaves:
consisting of title p. (i), verso blank; text pp. 1⁄35, p. 36 blank.

℃ Colored printer's device on title page and colored headpiece by Valenti An⁄
gelo. Type Lutetia, handset; paper Whatman. Bound in blue & gold decorated
boards with parchment back; title in gold on back. Two hundred and forty
copies printed for direct sale in April, 1927. Price $10.00.

℃ One of the Fifty Books of the Year.

94. A | LEGACY | OF | HOURS | BY | FLORA J. ARNSTEIN |
[design] | SAN FRANCISCO | 1927

7½ x 4¾. One blank leaf; pp. (i⁄ii); pp. 1⁄42; colophon: consisting of title p.
(i), copyright notice p. (ii), text pp. 1⁄42.

℃ Printer's device [F] below colophon. Type Caslon monotype; paper French
handmade. Bound in green boards; white label printed in green on front cover.
One hundred copies printed for Flora J. Arnstein in 1927.

[51]

42. The Grabhorn Press; San Francisco, California 1940
Elinor Raas Heller and David Magee, *Bibliography of the Grabhorn Press, 1915–1940*. 10 x 14
The Grabhorn Press. 210 copies, Goudy Franciscan type. [*see bibliography no. 30*]

43. Roger Lacourière (plates) and Marthe Fequet & Pierre Baudier (text); Paris, France   1942
G. L. de Buffon, *Eaux-Fortes Originales pour Textes de Buffon*, with etchings by Pablo Picasso. 11 x 14½
Martin Fabiani. 226 copies. [*see bibliography no. 12*]

44. Bauersche Giesserei; Frankfurt am Main, Germany   1943
Apokalypse, with illustrations by Max Beckmann. 11⅜ x 15⅜
Bauersche Giesserei. About 41 copies, Legend type. [*see bibliography no. 12*]

LA DAME DE PARIS

45. Roger Lacourière (plates) and Georges Girard (text); Paris, France   1943
François Rabelais, *Pantagruel*, with color woodcuts by André Derain. 11 x 13½
Albert Skira. 275 copies, Garamond type. [*see bibliography no. 22*]

ESTHÉTIQUE DU MAL

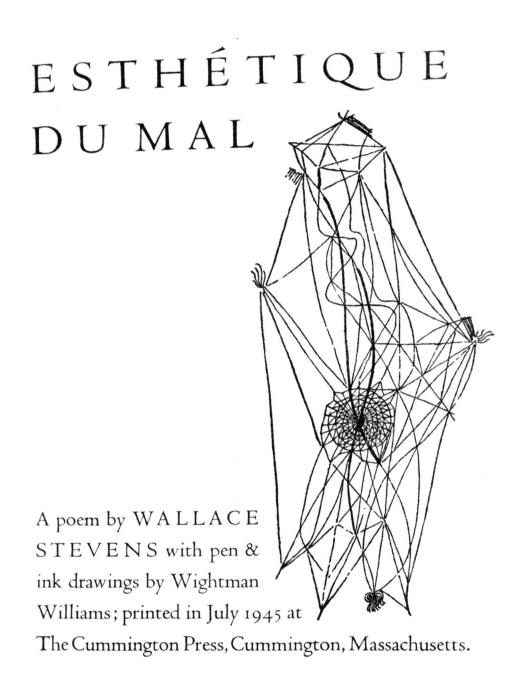

A poem by WALLACE
STEVENS with pen &
ink drawings by Wightman
Williams; printed in July 1945 at
The Cummington Press, Cummington, Massachusetts.

46. The Cummington Press (Harry Duncan); Cummington, Massachusetts   1945
Wallace Stevens, *Esthétique du Mal*, with drawings by Wightman Williams. 6½ x 9½
The Cummington Press. 340 copies, Centaur type. [*see bibliography no. 45*]

PSALM CXXVIII
A SONG OF DEGREES.

Blessed is every one that feareth the Lord; that walketh in his ways.

2. For thou shalt eat the labour of thine hands: happy shalt thou be, and it shall be well with thee.

3. Thy wife shall be as a fruitful vine by the sides of thine house: thy children like olive plants round about thy table.

4. Behold, that thus shall the man be blessed that feareth the Lord.

5. The Lord shall bless thee out of Zion: and thou shalt see the good of Jerusalem all the days of thy life.

6. Yea, thou shalt see thy children's children, and peace upon Israel.

PSALM CXXVIIII
A SONG OF DEGREES.

Many a time have they afflicted me from my youth, may Israel now say:

2. Many a time have they afflicted me from my youth: yet they have not prevailed against me.

3. The plowers plowed upon my back: they made long their furrows.

4. The Lord is righteous: he hath cut asunder the cords of the wicked.

47. Joh. Enschedé en Zonen (Jan van Krimpen); Haarlem, The Netherlands
The Book of Psalms. 5¾ x 9⅜
Stichtung De Roos. No limitation given, Romanée type. [*see bibliography no. 17*]

1947

48. Edward Vairel (plates) and Draeger Frères (text); Paris, France   1947
Henri Matisse, *Jazz*, with illustrations by Henri Matisse. 12½ x 16½
Tériade Éditeur. 270 copies, Matisse calligraphy. [*see bibliography no. 22*]

STUTTGART

An Siegfried Schmidt

I

Wieder ein Glück ist erlebt. Die gefährliche Dürre geneset,
    Und die Schärfe des Lichts senget die Blüte nicht mehr.
Offen steht jetzt wieder ein Saal, und gesund ist der Garten,
    Und von Regen erfrischt rauschet das glänzende Tal,
Hoch von Gewächsen, es schwellen die Bäch' und alle gebundnen
    Fittige wagen sich wieder ins Reich des Gesangs.
Voll ist die Luft von Fröhlichen jetzt, und die Stadt und der Hain ist
    Rings von zufriedenen Kindern des Himmels erfüllt.
Gerne begegnen sie sich, und irren untereinander,
    Sorgenlos, und es scheint keines zu wenig, zu viel.
Denn so ordnet das Herz es an, und zu atmen die Anmut,
    Sie, die geschickliche, schenkt ihnen ein göttlicher Geist.
Aber die Wanderer auch sind wohlgeleitet und haben
    Kränze genug und Gesang, haben den heiligen Stab
Vollgeschmückt mit Trauben und Laub bei sich und der Fichte
    Schatten; von Dorfe zu Dorf jauchzt es, von Tage zu Tag,
Und wie Wagen, bespannt mit freiem Wilde, so ziehn die
    Berge voran und so träget und eilet der Pfad.

II

Aber meinest du nun, es haben die Tore vergebens
    Aufgetan und den Weg freudig die Götter gemacht?
Und es schenken umsonst zu des Gastmahls Fülle die Guten
    Nebst dem Weine noch auch Blumen und Honig und Obst?
Schenken das purpurne Licht zu Festgesängen und kühl und
    Ruhig zu tieferem Freundesgespräche die Nacht?
Hält ein Ernsteres dich, so spars dem Winter und willst du
    Freien, habe Geduld, Freier beglücket der Mai.
Jetzt ist anderes not, jetzt komm und feire des Herbstes
    Alte Sitte, noch jetzt blühet die Edle mit uns.
Eins nur gilt für den Tag, das Vaterland und des Opfers
    Festlicher Flamme wirft jeder sein Eigenes zu,
Darum kränzt der gemeinsame Gott umsäuselnd das Haar uns,
    Und den eigenen Sinn schmelzet, wie Perlen, der Wein.

130

49. Stamperia del Santuccio (Victor Hammer); Lexington, Kentucky   1949
J. C. F. Hölderlin, *Gedichte.* 9 x 13
Stamperia del Santuccio. 51 copies, American Uncial type. [*see bibliography no. 31*]

Das größeste ist das Alphabet,
denn alle Weisheit steckt darin·
Aber nur der erkennt den Sinn,
der's recht zusammenzusetzen versteht·

Geibel

18

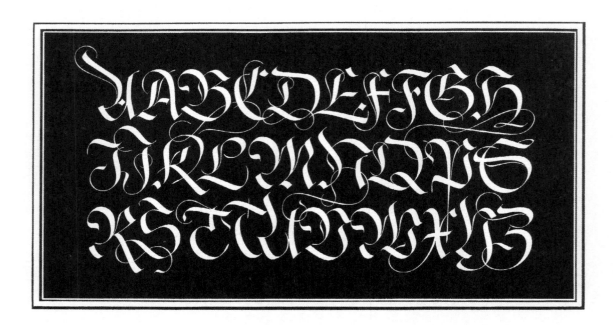

50. D. Stempel AG (Hermann Zapf); Frankfurt, Germany   1949
Hermann Zapf & August Rosenberger, *Feder und Stichel*. 12½ x 9⅛
D. Stempel AG. 500 copies on Fabriano paper, Palatino type with the author's calligraphic exemplars.
[*see bibliography no. 57*]

PAPERMAKING
BY HAND
IN
AMERICA

DARD HUNTER

CHILLICOTHE, OHIO
UNITED STATES OF AMERICA
MOUNTAIN HOUSE PRESS
Anno Domini 1950

51. Mountain House Press (Dard Hunter); Chillicothe, Ohio   1950
Dard Hunter, *Papermaking by Hand in America*. 11½ x 16½
Mountain House Press. 210 copies, Dard Hunter roman type. [*see bibliography no. 32*]

IOANNES·PICVS
MIRANDVLAN
VS·COMES·CON
CORDIAE ✐ORA
TIO·DE·HOMIN
IS·DIGNITATE·

52. Anvil Press (Victor Hammer); Lexington, Kentucky   1953
Pico della Mirandola, *Oratio de Hominis Dignitate.* 8½ x 11⅞
Anvil Press. 225 copies, Emerson and Garamond types. [*see bibliography no. 31*]

Avez-vous remarqué combien l'Y est une lettre pittoresque qui a des significations sans nombre? – L'arbre est un Y; l'embranchement de deux routes est un Y; le confluent de deux rivières est un Y; une tête d'âne ou de bœuf est un Y; un verre sur son pied est un Y; un lys sur sa tige est un Y; un suppliant qui lève les bras au ciel est un Y. Au reste cette observation peut s'étendre à tout ce qui constitue élémentairement l'écriture humaine. Tout ce qui est dans la langue démotique y a été versé par la langue hiératique. L'hiéroglyphe est la racine nécessaire du caractère. Toutes les lettres ont d'abord été des signes et tous les signes ont d'abord été des images. La société humaine, le monde, l'homme tout entier est dans l'alphabet. La maçonnerie, l'astronomie, la philosophie, toutes les sciences ont là leur point de départ, imperceptible, mais réel; et cela doit être. L'alphabet est une source. A, c'est le toit, le pignon avec sa traverse, l'arche, *arx*; ou c'est l'accolade de deux amis qui s'embrassent et qui se serrent la main; D, c'est le dos; B, c'est le D sur le D, le dos sur le dos, la bosse; C, c'est le croissant, c'est la lune; E, c'est le soubassement, le pied droit, la console et l'architrave, toute l'architecture à plafond dans une seule lettre; F, c'est la potence, la fourche, *furca*; G, c'est le cor; H, c'est la façade de l'édifice avec ses deux tours; I, c'est la machine de guerre lançant le projectile; J, c'est le soc et c'est la corne d'abondance; K, c'est l'angle de réflexion égal à l'angle d'incidence, une des cléfs de la géométrie; L, c'est la jambe et le pied; M, c'est la montagne, ou c'est le camp, les tentes accouplées; N, c'est la porte fermée avec sa barre diagonale; O, c'est le soleil; P, c'est le portefaix debout avec sa charge sur le dos; Q, c'est la croupe avec la queue; R, c'est le repos, le portefaix appuyé sur son bâton; S, c'est le serpent; T, c'est le marteau; U, c'est l'urne; V, c'est le vase (de là vient qu'on les confond souvent); je viens de dire ce que c'est qu'Y; X, ce sont les épées croisées, c'est le combat; qui sera vainqueur? on l'ignore; aussi les hermétiques ont-ils pris X pour le signe du destin, les algébristes pour le signe de l'inconnu; Z, c'est l'éclair, c'est Dieu. Ainsi, d'abord la maison de l'homme et son architecture, puis le corps de l'homme et sa structure et ses difformités; puis la justice, la musique, l'église; la guerre, la moisson, la géométrie; la montagne; la vie nomade, la vie cloîtrée; l'astronomie; le travail et le repos; le cheval et le serpent; le marteau et l'urne, qu'on renverse et qu'on accouple et dont on fait la cloche; les arbres, les fleuves, les chemins; enfin le destin et Dieu, – voilà ce que contient l'alphabet.

Next in importance to the type are the ornaments, initial letters, & other decorations which can be printed along with it. These, it is obvious, should always be designed & engraved so as to harmonize with the printed page regarded as a whole. — Emery Walker

53. D. Stempel AG (Hermann Zapf); Frankfurt, Germany   1954
Hermann Zapf, *Manuale Typographicum*. 12 x 9
D. Stempel AG / Museum Books. 1,000 copies, various types from the Stempel typefoundry. [*see bibliography no. 57*]

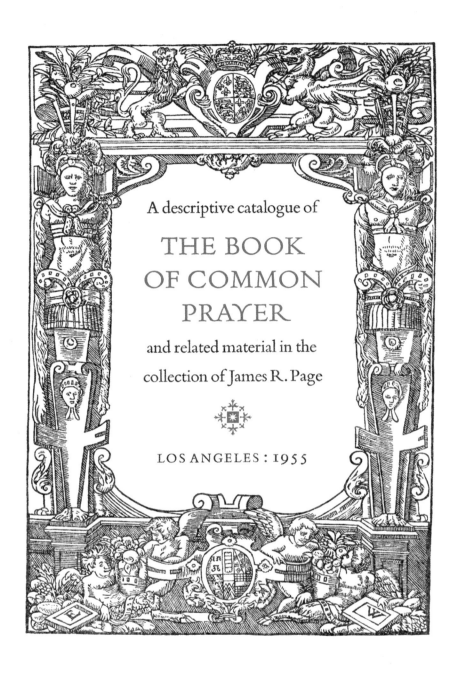

A descriptive catalogue of

THE BOOK
OF COMMON
PRAYER

and related material in the
collection of James R. Page

※

LOS ANGELES : 1955

54. The Plantin Press (Saul and Lillian Marks); Los Angeles, California   1955
James R. Page, *A Descriptive Catalogue of the Book of Common Prayer.* 8 x 11½
No limitation given, Bembo type. [*see bibliography no. 40*]

PSALMUS XVIII

Magistro chori. Psalmus. Davidis.

Caeli enarrant gloriam Dei,
et opus manuum eius annuntiat firmamentum.
Dies diei effundit verbum,
et nox nocti tradit notitiam.
Non est verbum et non sunt sermones,
quorum vox non percipiatur:
In omnem terram exit sonus eorum,
et usque ad fines orbis eloquia eorum.

Ibi posuit soli tabernaculum suum,
qui procedit ut sponsus de thalamo suo,
exsultat ut gigas percurrens viam.
A termino caeli fit egressus eius,
et circuitus eius usque ad terminum caeli,
nec quidquam subtrahitur ardori eius.

Lex Domini perfecta, recreans animam;
praescriptum Domini firmum, instituens rudem;
Praecepta Domini recta, delectantia cor;
mandatum Domini mundum, illustrans oculos;
Timor Domini purus, permanens in aeternum;
iudicia Domini vera, iusta omnia simul,
Desiderabilia super aurum et obryzum multum
et dulciora melle et liquore favi.

Etsi servus tuus attendit illis,
in iis custodiendis sedulus est valde,
Errata tamen quis animadvertit?
a mihi occultis munda me.
A superbia quoque prohibe servum tuum,
ne dominetur in me.
Tunc integer ero et mundus
a delicto grandi.
Accepta sint eloquia oris mei et meditatio cordis mei
coram te, Domine, Petra mea et Redemptor meus.

55. The St. Albert's Press (William Everson); San Francisco, California   1955
Novum Psalterium Pii XII, 10¼ x 15½
Dawson's Book Shop. 48 copies, Goudy Newstyle type. [*see bibliography no. 33*]

differentie al proposito satisfaccia. E de l'altre se dica.

De le pyramidi laterate e sue diversità. Capitulo LXV.

L E pyramidi laterate, excelso Duca, sonno de infinite sorte, sì commo le varietà de le lor colonne donde hano origine, commo apresso concluderemo. Ma prima del nostro philosopho poniamo sua dechiaratione nel suo 11° posta, dove dici la pyramide laterata esser una figura corporea [76r.] contenuta da le superficie, le quali da una in fore sonno elevate in su a un ponto opposto. El perchè è da notare che in ogni pyramide laterata tutte le superficie che la circundano, excepta la sua basa, se sulevano a un ponto el quale fia dicto cono de la pyramide; e tutte queste tali superficie laterali sonno triangole e al più de le volte la lor basa non è triangola, commo qui in linea apare la pyramide .A. triangola, de la quale el cono .B.; e la pyramide .D. quadrilatera e 'l suo cono .E.; e la pyramide pentagona .F. e 'l suo cono .G. E così sequendo, in tutte e meglio in sua propria forma materiale, a li numeri LI, LII, LIII, LIIII, LV, LVI, de solide e vacue e di sotto in questo, in piano per prospectiva a li medesimi numeri. E la derivatione de queste tali è da le colonne laterate de le quali sopra dicemmo, e nascano in questo modo, cioè fermando un ponto attualmente in una de le basi de la colonna laterata, overo imaginandolo, e quello congiongnendo per li-

LI
LII

125

56. Officina Bodoni (Giovanni Mardersteig); Verona, Italy   1956
Luca Pacioli, *De Divina Proportione.* 7⅞ x 11¼
Medio Banca di Milano. 280 copies, Bembo and Pacioli types. [*see bibliography no. 39*]

PRINTING
FOR
THEATER

BY
ADRIAN WILSON

SAN FRANCISCO : 1957

57. Adrian Wilson; San Francisco, California
Adrian Wilson, *Printing for Theater.* 10¼ x 15½
250 copies, Caslon and Trajanus types. [*see bibliography no. 55*]

Ce mouvement l'effraya; il me répondit que, si c'était ainsi que je le recevais lorsqu'il venait me rendre compte du service le plus considé-

rable qu'il eût pu me rendre, il allait se retirer et ne remettrait jamais le pied chez moi. Je courus à la porte de la chambre, que je fermai soigneusement.

— Ne t'imagine pas, lui dis-je en me tournant vers lui, que tu puisses me prendre encore une fois pour dupe et me tromper par des fables. Il faut défendre ta vie, ou me faire retrouver Manon.

— Là! que vous êtes vif! reprit-il; c'est l'unique sujet qui m'amène. Je viens vous annoncer un bonheur auquel vous ne pensez pas et pour lequel vous reconnaîtrez peut-être que vous m'avez quelque obligation.

Je voulus être éclairci sur-le-champ. Il me raconta que Manon, ne pouvant soutenir la crainte de la misère et surtout l'idée d'être obligée tout d'un coup à la réforme de notre équipage, l'avait prié

58. The Overbrook Press (Thomas Maitland Cleland), Stamford, Connecticut   1958
L'Abbé Prévost, *Histoire du Chevalier des Grieux et de Manon Lescaut*, with serigraphs by T. M. Cleland. 9 x 12
The Overbrook Press. 200 copies, Caslon type. [*see bibliography no. 10*]

OVID'S METAMORPHOSES

IN FIFTEEN BOOKS

★

TRANSLATED
INTO ENGLISH VERSE UNDER
THE DIRECTION OF SIR SAMUEL GARTH
BY JOHN DRYDEN, ALEXANDER POPE,
JOSEPH ADDISON, WILLIAM CONGREVE
AND OTHER EMINENT
HANDS

★

PRINTED FOR THE
MEMBERS OF THE LIMITED EDITIONS CLUB
AT THE OFFICINA BODONI IN VERONA
1958

59. Stamperia Valdonega (Giovanni Mardersteig); Verona, Italy   1958
Ovid, *Metamorphoses*, with etchings by Hans Erni. 6¼ x 9½
The Limited Editions Club. 1,500 copies, Centaur type. [*see bibliography no. 6*]

THE ALPHABET
IN VARIOUS
ARRANGEMENTS

60. The Hammer Creek Press (John Fass); New York, New York   1958
The Alphabet in Various Arrangements, 5¾ x 7¾
The Hammer Creek Press. 8 copies, various types. [*see bibliography no. 14*]

1 Im Anfang war das Wort, und das Wort war bei Gott, und Gott war das Wort. ²Dasselbe war im Anfang bei Gott. ³Alle Dinge sind durch dasselbe gemacht, und ohne dasselbe ist nichts gemacht, was gemacht ist. ⁴In ihm war das Leben, und das Leben war das Licht der Menschen. ⁵Und das Licht scheint in der Finsternis, und die Finsternis hat's nicht ergriffen.

⁶Es war ein Mensch, von Gott gesandt, der hieß Johannes. ⁷Der kam zum Zeugnis, daß er von dem Licht zeugte, auf daß sie alle durch ihn glaubten. ⁸Er war nicht das Licht, sondern er sollte zeugen von dem Licht.

⁹Das war das wahrhaftige Licht, welches alle Menschen erleuchtet, die in diese Welt kommen. ¹⁰Er war in der Welt, und die Welt ist durch ihn gemacht; aber die Welt erkannte ihn nicht. ¹¹Er kam in sein Eigentum; und die Seinen nahmen ihn nicht auf. ¹²Wie viele ihn aber aufnahmen, denen gab er Macht, Gottes Kinder zu werden, die an seinen Namen glauben, ¹³welche nicht von dem Geblüt noch von dem Willen des Fleisches noch von dem Willen eines Mannes, sondern von Gott geboren sind.

¹⁴Und das Wort ward Fleisch und wohnte unter uns, und wir sahen seine Herrlichkeit, eine Herrlichkeit als des eingebornen Sohnes vom Vater, voller Gnade und Wahrheit. ¹⁵Johannes zeugt von ihm, ruft und spricht: Dieser war es, von dem ich gesagt habe: Nach mir wird kommen, der vor mir gewesen ist; denn er war eher als ich. ¹⁶Und von seiner Fülle haben wir alle genommen Gnade um Gnade. ¹⁷Denn das Gesetz ist durch Mose gegeben; die Gnade und Wahrheit ist durch Jesus Christus geworden. ¹⁸Niemand hat Gott je gesehen; der eingeborne Sohn, der in des Vaters Schoß ist, der hat ihn uns verkündigt.

¹⁹Und dies ist das Zeugnis des Johannes, da die Juden zu ihm sandten von Jerusalem Priester und Leviten, daß sie ihn fragten: Wer bist du? ²⁰Und er bekannte und leugnete nicht, und er bekannte: Ich bin nicht der Christus. ²¹Und sie fragten ihn: Was denn? Bist du Elia? Er sprach: Ich bin's nicht. Bist du der Prophet? Und er antwortete: Nein. ²²Da sprachen sie zu ihm: Was bist du denn? daß wir Antwort geben denen, die uns gesandt haben. Was sagst du von dir selbst? ²³Er sprach: »Ich bin eine Stimme eines Predigers in der Wüste: Richtet den Weg des Herrn!« wie der Prophet Jesaja gesagt hat.

²⁴Und es kamen, die gesandt waren von den Pharisäern. ²⁵Die

Ἐν ἀρχῇ ἦν ὁ λόγος, καὶ ὁ λόγος ἦν πρὸς τὸν θεόν, καὶ θεὸς ἦν ὁ λόγος. οὗτος ἦν ἐν ἀρχῇ πρὸς τὸν θεόν. πάντα δι᾽ αὐτοῦ ἐγένετο, καὶ χωρὶς αὐτοῦ ἐγένετο οὐδὲ ἕν ὃ γέγονεν. ἐν αὐτῷ ζωὴ ἦν, καὶ ἡ ζωὴ ἦν τὸ φῶς τῶν ἀνθρώπων· καὶ τὸ φῶς ἐν τῇ σκοτίᾳ φαίνει, καὶ ἡ σκοτία αὐτὸ οὐ κατέλαβεν.

Ἐγένετο ἄνθρωπος, ἀπεσταλμένος παρὰ θεοῦ, ὄνομα αὐτῷ Ἰωάννης· οὗτος ἦλθεν εἰς μαρτυρίαν, ἵνα μαρτυρήσῃ περὶ τοῦ φωτός, ἵνα πάντες πιστεύσωσιν δι᾽ αὐτοῦ. οὐκ ἦν ἐκεῖνος τὸ φῶς, ἀλλ᾽ ἵνα μαρτυρήσῃ περὶ τοῦ φωτός.

Ἦν τὸ φῶς τὸ ἀληθινόν, ὃ φωτίζει πάντα ἄνθρωπον, ἐρχόμενον εἰς τὸν κόσμον. ἐν τῷ κόσμῳ ἦν, καὶ ὁ κόσμος δι᾽ αὐτοῦ ἐγένετο, καὶ ὁ κόσμος αὐτὸν οὐκ ἔγνω. εἰς τὰ ἴδια ἦλθεν, καὶ οἱ ἴδιοι αὐτὸν οὐ παρέλαβον. ὅσοι δὲ ἔλαβον αὐτόν, ἔδωκεν αὐτοῖς ἐξουσίαν τέκνα θεοῦ γενέσθαι, τοῖς πιστεύουσιν εἰς τὸ ὄνομα αὐτοῦ, οἳ οὐκ ἐξ αἱμάτων οὐδὲ ἐκ θελήματος σαρκὸς οὐδὲ ἐκ θελήματος ἀνδρὸς ἀλλ᾽ ἐκ θεοῦ ἐγεννήθησαν.

Καὶ ὁ λόγος σὰρξ ἐγένετο καὶ ἐσκήνωσεν ἐν ἡμῖν, καὶ ἐθεασάμεθα τὴν δόξαν αὐτοῦ, δόξαν ὡς μονογενοῦς παρὰ πατρός, πλήρης χάριτος καὶ ἀληθείας. Ἰωάννης μαρτυρεῖ περὶ αὐτοῦ καὶ κέκραγεν λέγων· οὗτος ἦν ὃν εἶπον· ὁ ὀπίσω μου ἐρχόμενος ἔμπροσθέν μου γέγονεν, ὅτι πρῶτός μου ἦν. ὅτι ἐκ τοῦ πληρώματος αὐτοῦ ἡμεῖς πάντες ἐλάβομεν, καὶ χάριν ἀντὶ χάριτος· ὅτι ὁ νόμος διὰ Μωϋσέως ἐδόθη, ἡ χάρις καὶ ἡ ἀλήθεια διὰ Ἰησοῦ Χριστοῦ ἐγένετο. Θεὸν οὐδεὶς ἑώρακεν πώποτε· μονογενὴς θεὸς ὁ ὢν εἰς τὸν κόλπον τοῦ πατρός, ἐκεῖνος ἐξηγήσατο.

Καὶ αὕτη ἐστὶν ἡ μαρτυρία τοῦ Ἰωάννου, ὅτε ἀπέστειλαν πρὸς αὐτὸν οἱ Ἰουδαῖοι ἐξ Ἱεροσολύμων ἱερεῖς καὶ Λευίτας ἵνα ἐρωτήσωσιν αὐτόν· σὺ τίς εἶ; καὶ ὡμολόγησεν καὶ οὐκ ἠρνήσατο, καὶ ὡμολόγησεν ὅτι ἐγὼ οὐκ εἰμὶ ὁ χριστός. καὶ ἠρώτησαν αὐτόν· τί οὖν; Ἠλίας εἶ σύ; καὶ λέγει· οὐκ εἰμί. ὁ προφήτης εἶ σύ; καὶ ἀπεκρίθη· οὔ. εἶπαν οὖν αὐτῷ· τίς εἶ; ἵνα ἀπόκρισιν δῶμεν τοῖς πέμψασιν ἡμᾶς· τί λέγεις περὶ σεαυτοῦ; ἔφη· ἐγὼ φωνὴ βοῶντος ἐν τῇ ἐρήμῳ· εὐθύνατε τὴν ὁδὸν κυρίου, καθὼς εἶπεν Ἡσαΐας ὁ προφήτης.

Καὶ ἀπεσταλμένοι ἦσαν ἐκ τῶν Φαρισαίων. καὶ ἠρώτησαν αὐτὸν καὶ εἶπαν αὐτῷ· τί

61. Trajanus Presse (Gotthard de Beauclair); Frankfurt, Germany   1960
Das Evangelium Johannes. 8 x 12¼
Trajanus Presse. 150 copies, Aldus and Heraklit (Greek) types. [*see bibliography no. 21*]

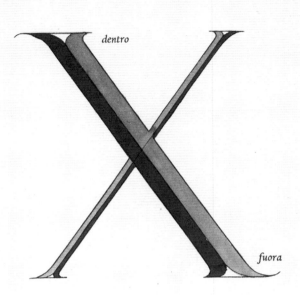

Considera oue le due linie si creano per lo ta-
gliare de la linia .×. con la circonferenza et in
quei puncti tira la littera .X.; mai poi ingrossa
vno decimo di fuora e dentro e testa la littera:
cossì farai del trauerso sutile secondo l'exemplo.

[XIv.]

62. Officina Bodoni (Giovanni Mardersteig); Verona, Italy   1960
Felice Feliciano (Giovanni Mardersteig, ed.), *Alphabetum Romanum*. 6 x 8⅞
Editiones Officinae Bodoni. 400 copies, Dante type. [*see bibliography no. 39*]

Diese Blümlein darff ich tragen

Mit mir hein / in mein Gezelt;

Aber dich mein Lieb zu fragen

Ob dir auch ein Kuß gefelt

Darff ich kaum mich unterstehen

Weil ich nie ein Bild gesehen

Das dir gleichet in der Welt.

1

63. Bauersche Giesserei; Frankfurt am Main, Germany   1961
Am Wegesrand, with woodcuts by Fritz Kredel. 7½ x 10½
Der Goldene Brunnen. 150 copies, Weiss roman type with calligraphy by George Salter. [*see bibliography no. 47*]

Karl Gruber

ASCHAFFENBURG
STADT ZWISCHEN SCHLOSS
UND STIFT

Mit einer kulturgeschichtlichen Betrachtung

von Wilhelm Hausenstein

Erschienen bei Hermann Emig Amorbach

1962

64. Ludwig Oehms (Hermann Zapf); Frankfurt, Germany   1962
Karl Gruber, *Aschaffenburg*. 4 x 6¾
Hermann Emig. No limitation given, Aldus and Palatino types. [*see bibliography no. 57*]

CHINESE

CALLIGRAPHY AND

PAINTING

IN THE COLLECTION OF

JOHN M. CRAWFORD, JR.

NEW YORK · 1962

65. The Spiral Press (Joseph Blumenthal); New York, New York
Laurence Sickman (ed.), *Chinese Calligraphy and Painting in the Collection of John M. Crawford, Jr.* 9¼ x 12¼
The Pierpont Morgan Library. 850 copies, Garamond and Sistina types. [*see bibliography no. 9*]

LES FABLES DE
JEAN DE LA FONTAINE

ILLUSTRÉES PAR
FRITZ KREDEL

66. D. Stempel AG (Hermann Zapf); Frankfurt, Germany   1963
Hermann Zapf, *Typographic Variations*. 8¼ x 12
Georg Kurt Schauer & Museum Books. 500 copies, Optima and assorted types from the Stempel typefoundry.
[*see bibliography no. 57*]

SEQUENCE

POEMS BY THEODORE ROETHKE

SOMETIMES
METAPHYSICAL

WITH WOOD ENGRAVINGS

BY JOHN ROY

THE STONE WALL PRESS, IOWA CITY

67. The Stone Wall Press (Kim Merker); Iowa City, Iowa   1963
Theodore Roethke, *Sequence, Sometimes Metaphysical*, with wood engravings by John Roy. 6⅞ x 10⅝
The Stone Wall Press. 330 copies, Romanée and Open Kapitalen types. [*see bibliography no. 7*]

as he came, so shall he go: and what profit hath he that hath laboured for the wind? All his days also he eateth in darkness, and he hath much sorrow and wrath with his sickness.

⁋ Behold that which I have seen: it is good and comely for one to eat and to drink, and to enjoy the good of all his labour that he taketh under the sun all the days of his life, which God giveth him: for it is his portion. Every man also to whom God hath given riches and wealth, and hath given him power to eat thereof, and to take his portion, and to rejoice in his labour; this is the gift of God. For he shall not much remember the days of his life; because God answereth him in the joy of his heart.

CHAPTER 6 There is an evil which I have seen under the sun, and it is common among men: A man to whom God hath given riches, wealth, and honour, so that he wanteth nothing for his soul of all that he desireth, yet God giveth him not power to eat thereof, but a stranger eateth it: this is vanity, and it is an evil disease.

⁋ If a man beget an hundred children, and live many years, so that the days of his years be many, and his soul be not filled with good, and also that he have no burial; I say, that an untimely birth is better than he. For he cometh in with vanity, and departeth in darkness, and his name shall be covered with darkness. Moreover he hath not seen the sun, nor known any thing: this hath more rest than the other.

⁋ Yea, though he live a thousand years twice told, yet hath he seen

68. The Spiral Press (Joseph Blumenthal); New York, New York
Ecclesiastes, with drawings by Ben Shahn. 9⅝ x 12⅞
The Spiral Press. 285 copies, Emerson type. [*see bibliography no. 9*]

1965

69. The Rampant Lions Press (Will Carter); Cambridge, England   1965
Armida Maria-Theresa Colt, *Weeds and Wildflowers*, with wood engravings by George Mackley. 9 x 11⅞
The Two-Horse Press. 250 copies, Arrighi type. [*see bibliography no. 11*]

70. Gehenna Press (Leonard Baskin); Northampton, Massachusetts   1967
Flosculi Sententiarum. 8 x 11½
Gehenna Press. 250 copies, Centaur type and assorted ornaments. [*see bibliography no. 5*]

Der Roman von Tristan und Isolde

ERNEUT VON JOSEPH BEDIER/IN DER ÜBERTRAGUNG

RUDOLF G. BINDINGS/MIT VIERZEHN HOLZSCHNITTEN

VON FRITZ KREDEL/EINE LIEBHABERAUSGABE DER

TRAJANUS-PRESSE ZU FRANKFURT AM MAIN

71. Trajanus Presse (Gotthard de Beauclair); Frankfurt, Germany   1966
Joseph Bédier (Rudolf G. Bindings, trans.), *Der Roman von Tristan und Isolde*, with woodcuts by Fritz Kredel. 6¾ x 10¾
Trajanus Presse. 300 copies, Sabon and Alte Schwabacher types. [*see bibliography no. 21*]

PRESSES

of the Pacific Islands

1817-1867

A history of the first half century
of printing in the Pacific islands

By RICHARD E. LINGENFELTER

Woodcuts by Edgar Dorsey Taylor

Los Angeles THE PLANTIN PRESS 1967

72. The Plantin Press (Saul and Lillian Marks); Los Angeles, California
Richard E. Lingenfelter, *Presses of the Pacific Islands 1817–1867.* 5¾ x 8¾
The Plantin Press. 500 copies, Bembo type. [*see bibliography no. 40*]

JOHN FELL

THE UNIVERSITY PRESS AND
THE 'FELL' TYPES

THE PUNCHES AND MATRICES DESIGNED FOR PRINTING
IN THE GREEK, LATIN, ENGLISH, AND ORIENTAL LANGUAGES
BEQUEATHED IN 1686 TO

THE UNIVERSITY OF OXFORD
BY JOHN FELL, D.D.

DELEGATE OF THE PRESS, DEAN OF CHRIST CHURCH
VICE-CHANCELLOR OF THE UNIVERSITY
AND BISHOP OF OXFORD

BY

STANLEY MORISON

WITH THE ASSISTANCE OF

HARRY CARTER

OXFORD
AT THE CLARENDON PRESS
MCMLXVII

73. Oxford University Press (Stanley Morison); Oxford, England   1967
Stanley Morison, *John Fell*. 10 x 14¾
Oxford, at the Clarendon Press. 1,000 copies, Fell types. [*see bibliography no. 2*]

C-S
The Master
Craftsman

An account of the work
of T. J. Cobden-Sanderson
by Norman H. Strouse

Cobden-Sanderson's
partnership with Emery Walker
by John Dreyfus

The Adagio Press
Harper Woods, Michigan
1969

74. The Adagio Press (Leonard Bahr); Harper Woods, Michigan   1969
Norman H. Strouse and John Dreyfus, *C-S The Master Craftsman*. 10 x 15⅛
The Adagio Press. 329 copies, Palatino and Pascal types. [*see bibliography no. 51*]

I

How vainly men themselves amaze
To win the Palm, the Oke, or Bayes;
And their uncessant Labours see
Crown'd from some single Herb or Tree,
Whose short and narrow verged Shade
Does prudently their Toyles upbraid;
While all Flow'rs and all Trees do close
To weave the Garlands of repose.

75. David R. Godine (David Godine and Lance Hidy); Boston, Massachusetts   1970
Andrew Marvell, *The Garden*, with etchings by Lance Hidy. 6⅜ x 9
David R. Godine. 115 copies, Cancelleresca Bastarda type.

76. Cherryburn Press (R. Hunter Middleton); Chicago, Illinois   1970
James M. Wells, *A Portfolio of Thomas Bewick Wood Engravings.* 8¼ x 10¼
The Newberry Library for the Cherryburn Press. 160 copies, Monotype Plantin type. [*see bibliography no. 56*]

77. The Trianon Press (Arnold Fawcus); Paris, France   1972
Geoffrey Keynes, *William Blake's Water-Colour Designs for the Poems of Thomas Gray.* 12⅞ x 16½
The Trianon Press for the William Blake Trust. Three volumes. 518 copies, Garamond type.

DE LUPO ET GRUE
.F. VIIII

78. Officina Bodoni (Giovanni Mardersteig); Verona, Italy   1973
The Fables of Aesop (William Caxton, trans.). 6½ x 9⅞
Editiones Officinae Bodoni. Two volumes, 160 copies, Centaur type. [*see bibliography no. 39*]

SIETE POEMAS SAJONES

JORGE LUIS BORGES

SEVEN SAXON POEMS

Impressions by ARNALDO POMODORO

Plain Wrapper Press

79. Plain Wrapper Press (Richard-Gabriel Rummonds and Alessandro Zanella); Verona, Italy   1974
Jorge Luis Borges, *Siete Poemas Sajones / Seven Saxon Poems*, with relief images by Arnaldo Pomodoro. 11⅜ x 15⅜
Plain Wrapper Press. 120 copies, Horizon type with calligraphy by Golda Fishbein. [*see bibliography no. 49*]

And wondered how the oracle had lied,
And wished her father knew it, and straightway
Rose up and clad herself. Slow went the day,
Though helped with many a solace, till came night;
And therewithal the new, unseen delight,
She learned to call her Love. 🍃 So passed away
The days and nights, until upon a day
As in the shade, at noon she lay asleep,
She dreamed that she beheld her sisters weep,
And her old father clad in sorry guise,
Grown foolish with the weight of miseries;
Her friends black-clad and moving mournfully,
And folk in wonder landed from the sea,
At such a fall of such a matchless maid,
And in her press apart her raiment laid
Like precious relics, and an empty tomb
Set in her palace telling of her doom.

31

80. The Rampant Lions Press (Will and Sebastian Carter); Cambridge, England   1974
William Morris, *The Story of Cupid and Psyche*, with illustrations by William Morris & Edward Burne-Jones. 9½ x 13⅝
Clover Hill Editions. Two volumes. 400 copies, Troy and Ehrhardt types. [*see bibliography no. 11*]

DAS SCHREIBBUCH DES VESPASIANO AMPHIAREO
VESPASIANO AMPHIAREO'S WRITING BOOK
VINEGIA · MDLIIII

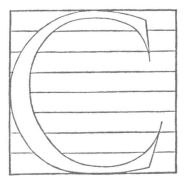

VOLLSTÄNDIGE NACHBILDUNG IN VOLLER GRÖSSE · HERAUSGEGEBEN VON JAN TSCHICHOLD

A COMPLETE FULL-SIZE REPRODUCTION · EDITED BY JAN TSCHICHOLD

DR.CANTZ'SCHE DRUCKEREI · STUTTGART-BAD CANNSTATT

81. Cantz'sche Druckerei, Stuttgart, Germany (Jan Tschichold; Berzona, Switzerland)   1975
Das Schreibbuch des Vespasiano Amphiareo (Jan Tschichold, ed.). 8⅜ x 6⅜
Dr. Cantz'sche Druckerei. 250 copies, Garamond type. [*see bibliography no. 35*]

TYPEFOUNDRIES
IN THE NETHERLANDS

FROM THE FIFTEENTH TO THE
NINETEENTH CENTURY

BY

CHARLES ENSCHEDÉ

A HISTORY BASED MAINLY
ON MATERIAL IN THE COLLECTION OF
JOH. ENSCHEDÉ EN ZONEN AT HAARLEM
FIRST PUBLISHED IN FRENCH IN 1908

AN ENGLISH TRANSLATION
WITH REVISIONS AND NOTES BY
HARRY CARTER
WITH THE ASSISTANCE OF
NETTY HOEFLAKE
EDITED BY
LOTTE HELLINGA

HAARLEM
STICHTING MUSEUM ENSCHEDÉ
1978

82. Joh. Enschedé en Zonen (Bram de Does); Haarlem, The Netherlands   1978
Charles Enschedé, *Typefoundries in the Netherlands* (Harry Carter, trans.) 10 x 15
Stichting Museum Enschedé. 1,550 copies, Romanée type with specimens from various types of the Enschedé typefoundry.

CHAPTER **I** LOOMINGS

ALL ME ISHMAEL.
Some years ago—never mind how long precisely—having little or no
money in my purse, and nothing particular to interest me on shore,
I thought I would sail about a little and see the watery part of the
world. It is a way I have of driving off the spleen, and regulating the
circulation. Whenever I find myself growing grim about the mouth;
whenever it is a damp, drizzly November in my soul; whenever I find
myself involuntarily pausing before coffin warehouses, and bringing
up the rear of every funeral I meet; and especially whenever my
hypos get such an upper hand of me, that it requires a strong moral
principle to prevent me from deliberately stepping into the street,
and methodically knocking people's hats off—then, I account it high
time to get to sea as soon as I can. This is my substitute for pistol and
ball. With a philosophical flourish Cato throws himself upon his
sword; I quietly take to the ship. There is nothing surprising in this.
If they but knew it, almost all men in their degree, some time or other,
cherish very nearly the same feelings towards the ocean with me.

2

83. Arion Press (Andrew Hoyem); San Francisco, California   1979
Herman Melville, *Moby-Dick; or, The Whale*, with wood engravings by Barry Moser. 10 x 15
Arion Press. 250 copies, Goudy Modern type.

The Allen Press Bibliography mcmlxxxi produced by hand with art work, sample pages from previous editions

84. The Allen Press (Lewis and Dorothy Allen); Greenbrae, California   1981
The Allen Press Bibliography. 9⅜ x 13⅞
The Allen Press. 140 copies, Romanée and Deepdene italic types. [*see bibliography no. 1*]

TRANSLATED BY W. S. MERWIN
FROM AN ANONYMOUS FRENCH
PLAY OF THE XIV CENTURY
WITH WOOD-ENGRAVINGS BY
ROXANNE SEXAUER

THE WINDHOVER PRESS AT
THE UNIVERSITY OF IOWA
IOWA CITY MCMLXXXI

85. The Windhover Press (Kim Merker); Iowa City, Iowa   1981
Anonymous, *Robert the Devil* (W. S. Merwin, trans.), with woodcuts by Roxanne Sexauer. 8⅞ x 12¾
The Windhover Press at the University of Iowa. 310 copies, Dante, Bembo italic, and Centaur types. [*see bibliography no. 7*]

THE REVELATION OF JESUS CHRIST,

which God gave unto him, to shew unto his servants
things which must shortly come to pass;
and he sent and signified it by his angel unto his servant John:
02 *Who bare record of the word of God, and of the testimony of Jesus Christ,*
and of all things that he saw.
03 *Blessed is he that readeth, and they that hear the words of this prophecy,*
and keep those things which are written therein: for the time is at hand.

JOHN

TO THE SEVEN CHURCHES WHICH ARE IN ASIA:

Grace be unto you, and peace, from him which is, and which was, and which is to come;
and from the seven Spirits which are before his throne;
05 And from Jesus Christ, who is the faithful witness,
and the first begotten of the dead, and the prince of the kings of the earth.
Unto him that loved us, and washed us from our sins in his own blood,
06 And hath made us kings and priests unto God and his Father;
to him be glory and dominion for ever and ever. Amen.
07 Behold, he cometh with clouds; and every eye shall see him, and they also which pierced him:
and all kindreds of the earth shall wail because of him. Even so, Amen.
08 ¶ I am Alpha and Omega, the beginning and the ending,
saith the Lord, which is, and which was, and which is to come, the Almighty.
09 ¶ I John, who also am your brother, and companion in tribulation,
and in the kingdom and patience of Jesus Christ,
was in the isle that is called Patmos,
for the word of God, and for the testimony of Jesus Christ.
10 I was in the Spirit on the Lord's day, and heard behind me a great voice, as of a trumpet,
11 Saying,

I am Alpha and Omega, the first and the last:

and,

What thou seest, write in a book, and send it unto the seven churches
which are in Asia; unto Ephesus, and unto Smyrna, and unto Pergamos,
and unto Thyatira, and unto Sardis, and unto Philadelphia, and unto Laodicea.
12 And I turned to see the voice that spake with me.
And being turned, I saw seven golden candlesticks;
13 And in the midst of the seven candlesticks one like unto the Son of man,
clothed with a garment down to the foot, and girt about the paps with a golden girdle.
14 His head and his hairs were white like wool, as white as snow;
and his eyes were as a flame of fire;

86. Arion Press (Andrew Hoyem); San Francisco, California 1982
Apocalypse: The Revelation of Saint John the Divine, with woodcuts by Jim Dine. 11 x 15
Arion Press. 150 copies, Garamond type. [*see bibliography no. 12*]

PAPERMAKING BY HAND

A BOOK OF SUSPICIONS BY WALTER HAMADY

THE PERISHABLE PRESS LIMITED

87. The Perishable Press Limited (Walter Hamady); Mount Horeb, Wisconsin   1982
Walter Hamady, *Papermaking by Hand.* 7⅛ x 11
The Perishable Press Limited. 200 copies, Palatino type with calligraphic title page by Hermann Zapf. [*see bibliography no. 26*]

The
Whittington
Press

A Bibliography 1971-1981

compiled by David Butcher

with an introduction and notes
by John Randle

The Whittington Press

88. The Whittington Press (John and Rosalind Randle); Andoversford, England — 1982
David Butcher and John Randle, *The Whittington Press: A Bibliography, 1971–1981.* 10⅜ x 14¾
The Whittington Press. 320 copies, Caslon type, with specimen pages printed in various types. [*see bibliography no. 43*]

C O M P A N Y

By Samuel Beckett

With 13 Etchings

By Dellas Henke

89. Iowa Center for the Book (Kim Merker); Iowa City, Iowa   1983
Samuel Beckett, *Company*, with etchings by Dellas Henke. 11¼ x 14
Iowa Center for the Book at the University of Iowa. 61 copies, Spectrum type. [*see bibliography no.* 7]

ALFRED STIEGLITZ

PHOTOGRAPHS & WRITINGS

Sarah Greenough

Juan Hamilton

NATIONAL GALLERY OF ART

Callaway Editions

90. Meriden-Stinehour Press (Eleanor Caponigro); Meriden, Connecticut & Lunenburg, Vermont   1983
Sarah Greenough and Juan Hamilton, *Alfred Stieglitz: Photographs & Writings*. 10½ x 14
National Gallery of Art and Callaway Editions. No limitation given, Bembo type. [*see bibliography no. 18*]

LO SPLENDORE DELLA VERONA AFFRESCATA

nelle tavole di Pietro Nanin del 1864

*Facsimile dell'unica raccolta colorata
con itinerari immaginari narrati da Nino Cenni
e uno studio sugli affreschi e i loro autori
di Gunter Schweikhart*

EDIZIONI VALDONEGA · VERONA

91. Stamperia Valdonega (Martino Mardersteig); Verona, Italy   1983
Pietro Nanin, *Lo Splendore della Verona affrescata*. 12½ x 17½
Edizioni Valdonega. 1,200 copies, Dante type. [*see bibliography no. 34*]

Frankenstein;

OR,

THE MODERN PROMETHEUS.

IN THREE VOLUMES.

Did I request thee, Maker, from my clay
To mould me man? Did I solicit thee
From darkness to promote me?————

PARADISE LOST.

VOL. III.

PENNYROYAL

92. Pennyroyal Press (Barry Moser); Northampton, Massachusetts   1983
Mary Shelley, *Frankenstein; or, The Modern Prometheus*, with wood engravings by Barry Moser. 10 x 13½
Pennyroyal Press. 350 copies, Poliphilus and Wilhelm Klingsporschrift types.

CHARLES G. FINNEY

The Circus of Doctor Lao

WITH RELIEF ETCHINGS BY CLAIRE VAN VLIET

THE JANUS PRESS VERMONT 1984

93. The Janus Press (Claire Van Vliet); Newark, Vermont   1984
Charles G. Finney, *The Circus of Dr. Lao*, with relief etchings by Claire Van Vliet. 10¼ x 13¼
The Janus Press. 150 copies, Plantin and Helvetica types. [*see bibliography no. 19*]

William Henry Fox Talbot   *A Scene in a Library*. c. 1844

94. Gilman Paper Company (Richard Benson and Martino Mardersteig) Newport, Rhode Island, and Verona, Italy   1985
Photographs from the Collection of the Gilman Paper Company. 15⅛ x 17⅞
White Oak Press. 1,200 copies, Bembo type.

FLOREAT
TYPOGRAPHIA

TYPOGRAPHIS · GENTIVM · OMNIVM
NON · ANTEA · LAVDATIS · SERMONE · HOC
COMMVNI · SALVTEM · DICIMVS
PLVRIMAM · OPTAMVSQVE · VT · ARS
VIGEAT · TYPOGRAPHICA
VNANIMAMQVE · INTER · GENTES
TOTIVS · ORBIS · TERRARVM
CONCORDIAM · FOVEAT

«MONOTYPE» PERPETUA, SERIE 258   PRINTED IN SWITZERLAND

95. Technische Hochschule Darmstadt, Darmstadt, Germany (Max Caflisch, Bern, Switzerland)   1988
Various authors, *Max Caflisch: Typographia Practica*. 8½ x 12½
Maximilian-Gesellschaft. 1,200 copies, various types.

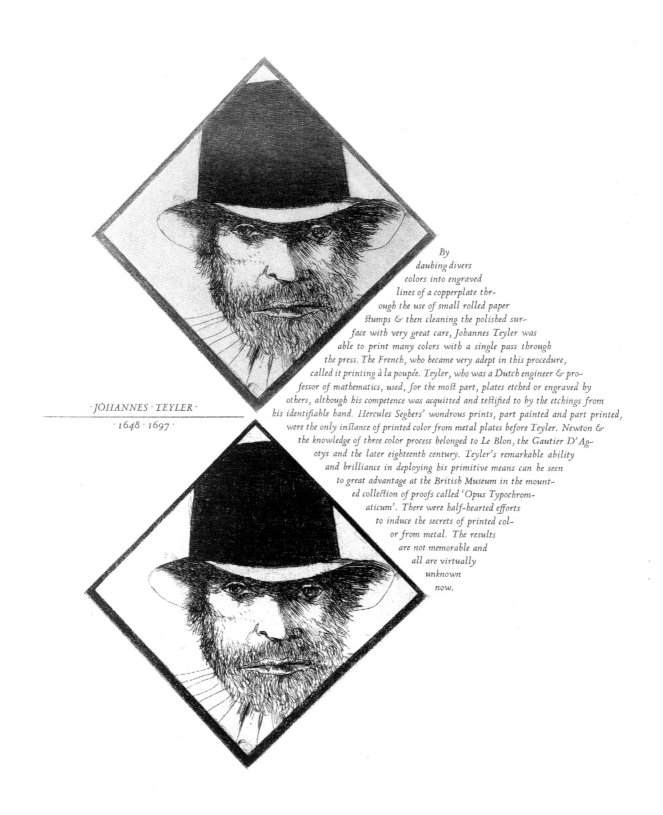

·JOHANNES·TEYLER·
·1648·1697·

By
daubing divers
colors into engraved
lines of a copperplate through the use of small rolled paper
stumps & then cleaning the polished surface with very great care, Johannes Teyler was
able to print many colors with a single pass through
the press. The French, who became very adept in this procedure,
called it printing à la poupée. Teyler, who was a Dutch engineer & pro-
fessor of mathematics, used, for the most part, plates etched or engraved by
others, although his competence was acquitted and testified to by the etchings from
his identifiable hand. Hercules Seghers' wondrous prints, part painted and part printed,
were the only instance of printed color from metal plates before Teyler. Newton &
the knowledge of three color process belonged to Le Blon, the Gautier D'Ag-
otys and the later eighteenth century. Teyler's remarkable ability
and brilliance in deploying his primitive means can be seen
to great advantage at the British Museum in the mounted collection of proofs called 'Opus Typochrom-
aticum'. There were half-hearted efforts
to induce the secrets of printed col-
or from metal. The results
are not memorable and
all are virtually
unknown
now.

96. Gehenna Press (Leonard Baskin); Leeds, Massachusetts   1988
Leonard Baskin, *Icones Librorum Artifices*, with etchings by Leonard Baskin. 11¼ x 16
Gehenna Press. 40 copies, Centaur and Arrighi types. [*see bibliography no. 5*]

WHAT is he up to, Gellius? what itch is he scratching 88
    in naked vigil there with his mother & sister?
what is the man up to, making his own uncle a cuckold?
    Have you any idea how great a sin he's committing?
—so great a sin that neither the waters of outermost Tethys
    nor Oceanus, father of Nymphs, could wash it away.
What worse could he stoop to, a man so thoroughly wicked?
    suck his own cock? No, that would be an improvement.

GELLIUS is lean—but of course: with such an obliging 89
    mother
    (so hale & hearty!) such a venerious sister,
an uncle who's also obliging, and so many girlfriends
    (all kissing cousins!) how could he possibly fatten?
Why, even if he had relations just with relations,
    you'd find no end of reasons there for his leanness.

FROM those unholy deeds which Gellius does with his 90
    mother,
    let a Magus be born & brought up to tell fortunes,
for if we can trust the outrageous religion of Persia
    a Magus must come from an incestuous couple,
so he may honor the gods with sweet hymns to their liking,
    and render in flames the fatty bowels of slain beasts.

REALLY now, Gellius, I didn't think I could trust you 91
    in this unhappy affair, this wretched business
on the grounds that I knew you well, or thought you were loyal,
    or able to keep yourself from malicious mischief:

90

97. Abattoir Editions (Harry Duncan); Omaha, Nebraska   1989
The Poems of Catullus. (Charles Martin, trans.), 6½ x 10
Abattoir Editions. 250 copies, Joanna and Romulus Open types. [*see bibliography no. 45*]

DAVID BUTCHER

The Stanbrook Abbey Press

1956-1990

WITH AN INTRODUCTION BY

JOHN DREYFUS

AND A MEMOIR OF DAME HILDELITH CUMMING BY

THE ABBESS OF STANBROOK

The Whittington Press

98. The Whittington Press (John and Rosalind Randle); Herefordshire, England   1992
David Butcher, *The Stanbrook Abbey Press 1956–1990*. 9 x 12½
The Whittington Press. 350 copies, Romulus type, with specimens set in various types. [*see bibliography no. 43*]

ORNAMENTED

TWENTY-THREE ALPHABETS FROM THE FOUNDRY OF LOUIS JOHN POUCHÉE

INTRODUCTION
JAMES MOSLEY

I. M. IMPRIMIT
IN ASSOCIATION WITH THE
ST BRIDE PRINTING LIBRARY
MCMXCIII

99. I. M. Imprimit (Ian Mortimer); London, England   1993
James Mosley, *Ornamented Types.* 15 x 21
I. M. Imprimit in association with the St Bride Printing Library. 200 copies, Scotch roman type.

A little apple half red, half yellow
Speaks of rose and saffron colors.

When a lover and a beloved part
The beloved keeps the adoration, the lover the pain.

The two opposing colors of that parting
Appear on both faces of love.

Yellow does not suit the beloved
Red's abundance and glow turn cold on the lover.

So when your lover spurns you
Endure it, do not battle.

Remember the heart is born from the body, and rules it
Like a man born from a woman.

Yet within the heart are the inner chambers
Like a rider hidden in a cloud of dust.

The movement of the dust comes from the rider
Who causes it to dance about.

No game can be started without thought
So you must throw the dice with conviction.

Shams is a sun within the heart
Whose warmth ripens the fruits at our core.

100. Wild Carrot Letterpress (Vincent FitzGerald and Jerry Kelly); Hadley, Massachusetts   1996
Jalaluddin Mohammad Rumi, *Divan-E-Shams* (Zahra Partovi, trans.), with illustrations in assorted media by twenty-two artists. 12½ x 14½
Vincent FitzGerald & Company. 50 copies, Zapf Renaissance type with calligraphy by Jerry Kelly. [*see bibliography no. 50*]

BIBLIOGRAPHY
&
INDICES

SELECTED BIBLIOGRAPHY

Listed are selected publications for further information on the books in this catalogue. Only one book per press is listed, selected for being the most complete or most recent reference for the book[s] included in this exhibition.

1. Allen, Lewis and Dorothy: *The Allen Press Bibliography: A Facsimile with original leaves & additions to date.*
   The Book Club of California, San Francisco, 1985.

2. Appleton, Tony: *The Writings of Stanley Morison.*
   Tony Appleton, Brighton, England, 1976.

3. Asaf, Alan: *Publications of the Grolier Club, 1884–1983.*
   The Grolier Club, New York, New York, 1984.

4. Ashendene Press (C. H. St. John Hornby): *A Descriptive Bibliography of the Books Printed at the Ashendene Press, MDCCCXCV–MCMXXXV.*
   Shelley House, Chelsea, England 1932.

5. Baskin, Lisa Unger: *The Gehenna Press / The Work of Fifty Years: 1942–1992.*
   The Bridwell Library & The Gehenna Press, 1992.

6. Beaujon, Paul, Paul A. Bennett, Edward Alden Jewell, James Laver & Thomas Craven: *Quarto-Millenary / The First 250 Publications and the First 25 Years / 1929–1954 / of the Limited Editions Club.*
   The Limited Editions Club, New York, New York, 1959.

7. Berger, Sidney E.: *Printing & the Mind of Merker: A Bibliographical Study.*
   The Grolier Club, New York, New York, 1997.

8. Berlincourt, Alain, et al.: *Max Caflisch / Typographia Practica.*
   Maximilian-Gesellschaft, Hamburg, Germany, 1988.

9. Blumenthal, Joseph: *The Spiral Press Through Four Decades.*
   The Pierpont Morgan Library, New York, New York, 1966.

10. Cahoon, Herbert: *The Overbrook Press Bibliography: 1934–1959.*
    The Overbrook Press, Stamford, Connecticut, 1963.

11. Carter, Will and Sebastian: *The Rampant Lions Press / A Printing Workshop through Five Decades.*
    The Rampant Lions Press, Cambridge, England, 1982.

12. Castleman, Riva: *A Century of Artists' Books.*
    The Museum of Modern Art, New York, New York, 1994.

13. Cobden-Sanderson, T.J.: *Catalogue Raisonné of Books Printed and Published at the Doves Press, 1900–1916.*
    Doves Press, Hammersmith, England, 1916.

14. Cohen, Herman, Jackson Burke, & Eugene M. Ettenberg: *John S. Fass & The Hammer Creek Press.*
    Melbert B. Cary, Jr. Graphic Arts Collection, Cary Library, Rochester Institute of Technology, Rochester, New York, 1998.

15. *The Colophon, The Annual of Book-Making.*
    The Colophon, New York, New York, 1938.

16. Dreyfus, John: *A History of The Nonesuch Press.*
    The Nonesuch Press, London, England, 1981.

17. Dreyfus, John: *The Work of Jan van Krimpen.*
    Sylvan Press, London, England, 1952.

18. Farrell, David: *The Stinehour Press: A Bibliographical Checklist of the First Thirty Years.*
    Meriden-Stinehour Press, Lunenburg, Vermont, 1988.

19. Fine, Ruth E.: *The Janus Press 1981–1990.*
    University of Vermont Libraries, Burlington, 1992.

20. Fine, Ruth E., William Matheson, and W. Thomas Taylor: *Printers' Choice.*
    W. Thomas Taylor, Austin, Texas, 1983.

21. Fischer, Gert, and Hans Richter: *Gotthard de Beauclair / Buchgestalter, Lyriker, Verlerger: 1907–1992.*
    Rheinlander Verlag, Siegberg, Germany, 1996.

22. Garvey, Eleanor: *The Artist & The Book: 1860–1960.*
    Museum of Fine Arts, Boston, Massachusetts, 1961.

23. Gill, Evan R.: *Bibliography of Eric Gill.*
    Cassell and Co., Limited, London, England, [1953].

24. Guggenheim, Siegfried: "Rudolf Koch," *Print*, vol. 5, no. 1.
    William E. Rudge, Woodstock, 1947.

25. Haas, Irvin: *Bruce Rogers: A Bibliography.*
    Peter Pauper Press, Mount Vernon, New York, 1936.

26. Hamady, Walter: *Two Decades of Hamady & The Perishable Press Limited.*
    University of Missouri, St. Louis, 1984.

27. Harlan, Robert D.: *John Henry Nash: The Biography of a Career.*
    University of California Press, Berkeley and Los Angeles and London, England, 1970.

28. Harrop, Dorothy A.: *A History of the Gregynog Press.*
    The Private Libraries Association, Pinner, Middlesex, England, 1980.

29. Hatch, Benton L.: *A Checklist of the Publications of Thomas Bird Mosher of Portland, Maine: MDCCCXCI–MDCCCCXXIII.*
    The University of Massachusetts Press, Amherst, 1966.

30. Heller, Elinor Rass, and David Magee: *Bibliography of the Grabhorn Press, 1916–40.*
    Grabhorn Press, San Francisco, California, 1940.

31. Holbrook, Paul: *Victor Hammer: Artist and Printer.*
    The Anvil Press, Lexington, Kentucky, 1981.

32. Hunter, Dard II, and Dard Hunter III: *Dard Hunter & Son.*
    Bird & Bull Press, Newtown, Pennsylvania, 1998.

33. Karmiole, Kenneth, and Sandra D. Kirschenbaum: *California Printing/Part III/1925–1975.*
    Book Club of California, San Francisco, 1987.

34. Kelly, Jerry: *The Officina Bodoni and the Stamperia Valdonega.*
    The Grolier Club, New York, New York, 1982.

35. Klemke, Werner: *Leben und Werk des Typographen Jan Tschichold.*
    Verlag Der Kunst, Dresden, Germany, [1977].

36. *The Lakeside Press: Ten Years of Bookmaking.*
    R. R. Donnelley & Sons, Chicago, Illinois, [n.d.].

37. Lehnacker, Josef, Herbert Post, Rudolf Adolph: *Die Bremer Presse.*
    Typographische Gesellschaft, München, Germany, 1964.

38. Magee, David and Dorothy: *Bibliography of the Grabhorn Press, 1940–56.*
    Grabhorn Press, San Francisco, California, 1957.

39. Mardersteig, Giovanni, and Hans Schmoller: *The Officina Bodoni/An Account of the Work of a Hand Press: 1923–1977.*
    Edizioni Valdonega, Verona, Italy, 1980.

40. Marks, Lillian: *Saul Marks & The Plantin Press.*
    The Plantin Press, Los Angeles, California, 1985.

41. McLean, Ruari: *Jan Tschichold Typographer.*
    Lund Humphreys, [London, England], [1975?].

42. Müller-Krumbach, Renate: *Harry Graf Kessler und Die Cranach-Presse in Weimar.*
    Maximilian-Gesellschaft, Hamburg, Germany, 1969.

43. Randle, John, John Dreyfus, and Mark Batty: *Printing at The Whittington Press: 1972–1994.*
    The Grolier Club, The Typophiles, and International Typeface Corporation, New York, New York, 1994.

44. Rathé, John F.: *Bibliography of the Typophile Chap Books, 1935–1992.*
    The Typophiles, New York, New York, 1992.

45. Richmond, Mary L.: "The Cummington Press" in *Books at Iowa: #7,* November 1967.
    University of Iowa Libraries, Iowa City, 1967.

46. Rudge, William E.: "George W. Jones," *Print,* vol. 3, no. 3.
    William E. Rudge, Woodstock, New York, 1943.

47. Schauer, Georg Kurt: *Deutsche Buchkunst: 1890 bis 1960.*
    Maximilian-Gesellschaft, Hamburg, Germany, 1963.

48. Simon, Herbert: *Song and Words: A History of the Curwen Press.*
    David R. Godine, Publisher, Boston, Massachusetts, 1973.

49. Smyth, Elaine, and Decherd Turner: *Plain Wrapper Press 1966–1988*.
W. Thomas Taylor, Austin, Texas, 1993.

50. Stein, Donna: *Vincent FitzGerald & Company: 1981–1992*.
Vincent FitzGerald & Company, New York, New York, 1992.

51. Tanner, Wesley B., and Eric C. Alstrom: *Adagio: A Checklist*.
Special Collections Library, University of Michigan, Ann Arbor, 1993.

52. Updike, D. B.: *Notes on the Merrymount Press and Its Work* (with bibliography by Julian Pearce Smith).
Harvard University Press, Cambridge, Massachusetts, 1934.

53. Urbanelli, Lora: *The Book Art of Lucien Pissarro*.
Moyer Bell, Kingston, Rhode Island and London, England, [1997].

54. Warde, Frederic: *Bruce Rogers: Designer of Books*.
Harvard University Press, Cambridge, Massachusetts, 1925.

55. Wilson, Adrian: *The Work & Play of Adrian Wilson*.
W. Thomas Taylor, Austin, Texas, 1983.

56. Young, Bruce, and Bruce Beck (eds.): *RHM: Robert Hunter Middleton, The Man and His Letters*.
Caxton Club, Chicago, Illinois, 1995.

57. *Hermann Zapf/Ein Arbeitsbericht*.
Maximilian-Gesellschaft, Hamburg, Germany, 1984.

AUTHORS & TITLES

DESIGNERS & PRESSES

PRINTED FROM GIOVANNI MARDERSTEIG'S DANTE TYPE
ON COUGAR OPAQUE NATURAL PAPER.
DESIGNED BY JERRY KELLY.